Becoming Change Makers

The Exquisite Path to Leadership and Liberation for Women of Color

Dominica McBride, PhD
& The BECOME Community

Net worlding
PUBLISHING

Praise for Becoming Change Makers

"Touching, empowering and raw, Dr. McBride takes you on a journey from trauma to triumph, beautifully woven from stories of resilience, recovery and restoration."

— NYC Independent

"This book is a courageous exploration and collection of wisdom that invites Women of Color to break through and harness your power for change."

— DC Chronicle

"A crucial and transformative journey for all women of color; an eye-opening and thought provoking read for everyone else."

— Los Angeles Tribune

"An honest and insightful look at intersectionality, power dynamics and how to become the leader necessary for real change today."

— London Digest

"This book has the power to catalyze women across generations, to create ripples of change that are needed in our communities, corporations and society."

— Seattle Independent

To Stafford L. Hood

Stafford was not only a teacher, but also a mentor, collaborator, co-creator, and friend. He was the forerunner of Culturally Responsive Evaluation and taught and immersed me in the joys at the intersection of community, culture, and context. This book would not exist without his foundational teaching.

Contents

Foreword

Exquisite is a word of great depth, evoking beauty, pleasure, and pain. Its roots lay in a careful selection and intent to create something exceptional. Our life journey is peppered with memorable moments, both joyous and sorrowful. Women of color experience a spectrum of extreme experiences on both ends, creating opportunities for personal transformation and community building.

Traditionally, leadership is seen as an embodiment of male energy, rooted in strength and perseverance. However, I believe that melanated women have a unique capacity to lead by combining feminine (yin) and masculine (yang) energies seamlessly, which touch hearts in ways that are unparalleled. We draw strength from our heritage, and our tribal mindset is rooted in the resilience our ancestors imbibed. Incorporating this energy into our leadership revives our culture and spirit, helping us to create lasting change.

We possess a divine creativity that moves with grace, strength and protection. It's a power that unfurls in a symphony of soft silk and mighty bear roars. This collection of one-on-one interviews with thirteen remarkable women captures the life-altering events that led to leadership.

Immerse yourself in their stories and be inspired.

Dominica McBride, PhD

Prologue

The journey of leadership has stretched me, molded me, tapped me, and transformed me. It has created, evoked, and inspired ideas and pushed me into shadows of what I have wanted to avoid within. The change makers that have come before have paved the way for us to create even greater and lasting change now – we can be guided by their examples, through their triumphs and mistakes, and step higher onto the foundation they formed.

Come. Reflect. Listen to and follow both the voices coming through the pages and also to your own authentic voice, your heart. This is an invitation and tool for your journey to step into your more liberated, empowered, and higher self – your change making power. You are needed now just as much—if not more—than at any other time in history. Women of color, with our life experiences at the intersection of societal oppression and empathetic resilience, are the conduits for the healing that our societies so desperately need.

As we emerge from the collective trauma of a global pandemic, civic uprising, economic hardship, and profound loss, many of us continue to carry the scars of those experiences. They were before unimaginable, but we have lived through them—and we continue

1

to endure them. Yet, amid this suffering, we are called to heal. We are called to liberate ourselves from the weight of these burdens. And we, as melanated women, hold a unique power. When we step into our authentic, loving, and liberated selves, we are not just surviving—we are answering the call to restore and recover society itself.

But stepping into this potential, this destiny, requires an unveiling —a deep, personal recovery and restoration. It is the path to healing, for healing cannot exist without acknowledging our pain. This is a reminder that liberation starts from within.

Since first publishing this book in September of 2023, there have continued to be awe-inspiring feats achieved by women of color, demonstrating the immense power and continued legacy of leadership rooted in authenticity. On July 21st, 2024, I stood on my mother's porch, gazing out at a string of mountains covered in looming trees and streams slipping in between, when I heard the news that President Biden was stepping out of the 2024 Presidential race, passing the torch to then Vice President Kamala Harris. Her rise as the first Black woman and first South Asian woman to run for this highest office in U.S. politics marked a monumental shift in what political success and leadership could look like.

In the same year, at the 2024 Summer Olympics, we saw the continued brilliance of women of color. Lauren Scruggs earned a silver medal in women's individual foil, and Simone Biles again claimed gold, solidifying her legacy as one of the greatest athletes of all time. At the World Championships, Marileidy Paulino became the first woman from the Dominican Republic to win an individual title, reminding us of the power of perseverance and the pride of heritage.

This is not merely about their victories; it is about what they represent. Each of these women stepped into spaces not always designed for them, and they flourished. They became symbols of what is possible when we embrace our highest potential, unafraid to break through the boundaries that have long been set before us. These achievements are a testament to the rising tide of women of color claiming their rightful place in leadership.

Women like Beyoncé, who transcended musical genres with her release of a country album, defying expectations and showcasing the vastness of Black women's contributions to music, and Laphonza Butler, appointed to the U.S. Senate on October 2, 2023, becoming the first Black lesbian to serve in this capacity. Alexandria Ocasio-Cortez continues to lead boldly, amplifying her political voice, and inspiring people far beyond her congressional district.

Each of these leaders has shown that leadership, at its core, is about stepping fully into one's power, potential, and "authentic swing." It's about embracing the intersectionality of our identities —where we come from, what we've endured, and what we believe in—and using that to fuel our impact. The power and potential of women of color in leadership are undeniable, and I expect even greater things to occur when you step into—or amplify—yours.

As you move through this book, take time to reflect, journey with others, and fuel yourself with the insights you gather. This is a moment to consider your own leadership, whether it is in the past, present, or yet to come, regardless of position or title. It's a time to embrace your power and potential—not just for yourself but for your community. True leadership requires risk, courage, and stepping outside of your comfort zone.

Through this journey, I urge you to become an even bolder version of yourself. Let this be the moment when you explore and discover both the old and new aspects of who you are. Our stories are our strength. The struggles we've faced, the resilience we've shown—these are the building blocks of our leadership. Embrace your story, honor your heritage, and step forward with the knowledge that you are a necessary part of the change we seek in this world.

Becoming Change Makers

You, too, are a change maker. Whether you realize it or not, your life, your voice, and your presence are shaping the world around you. And now, more than ever, the world needs your light. Step into your authenticity, and lead with love, purpose, and balanced power. Together, we will rise.

Introduction

How and When This Book Was Born

"Say it. Say parsley," the soldier demanded. He fingered the blade of his blood-stained machete while he waited. The year was 1937, and the setting was somewhere in Haiti. Driven by long-standing racial tensions, political instability, and economic competition between Haiti and the Dominican Republic, Dominican dictator Rafael Trujillo ordered the mass killing of Haitians and people of Haitian descent. His decree included anyone living along the border between the two countries.

"Say parsley" was a simple but gruesome method soldiers used to identify potential Haitians. Dominican soldiers would hold up a sprig of parsley and ask individuals to pronounce the Spanish word for parsley, *perejil*.

Because the Haitian Creole accent made it difficult to pronounce the Spanish word correctly, those who failed the test were executed on the spot, either slashed and stabbed to death with machetes, shot, forcefully drowned, or beaten to death.

Trujillo had basically put a hit out on any Haitians that were within the Dominican Republic. Not one to hide or flee, my grandfather headed up a rescue mission for Haitians along the border to bring them to safety so they wouldn't be killed or maimed by Trujillo's death squads. Every time I remember the story, or share it with people, his actions still make me shiver.

Although an estimated 15,000 to 30,000 Haitians were killed, their resistance and courage is yet another devastating and heroic example of their cultural strength. The Haitian Revolution, a major anti-slavery and anti-colonial uprising that lasted from 1791 to 1804, was the first example that I became aware of. Ultimately, their struggle led to the establishment of an independent nation, and Haiti became the first country in the world to fight and become free of slavery. Haiti—my history, my heritage.

I'm very proud that the courage, resilience, and fight my grandfather had now courses through my blood—literally, through the science of epigenetics, I have his DNA in me. When I say "I honor my culture," that's core to what I'm talking about.

Some people assume *culture* means ethnic food or clothing, your accent, where you grew up, the music you listened to, or the art you create or appreciate.

I believe those things matter, but real culture is also the parts of your ancestors that made them who they were—warriors, family members, fathers, mothers, and freedom seekers who in turn shape what you are today. Culture is your roots, where you came from, what you're made of, and what matters to you.

When I say "this book was born before I was," I mean it was born in my ancestors and all they endured. It was born in how they handed down their stories and songs, and trauma in sharing how they became free.

Thousands of Haitians and Dominicans of Haitian descent were brutally murdered or forcibly expelled from the Dominican

Introduction

Republic during that onslaught. Many, like those my grandfather led, escaped, but were displaced.

This violence and the displacement of Haitians intensified the hostility between the two nations. That animosity lasts to this day in terms of diplomatic and social relations. Despite all that happened, my grandfather had daughters and they were born with his DNA, including my mom—a bright and amazingly resilient woman, and passed it down to me. He survived and so does his story.

The Parsley Massacre itself remains a painful and traumatic chapter in both countries' histories. Even today, it stands as a tragic example of ethnic violence and discrimination. Yet, for me, it represents something more valuable and powerful.

I was born from those Haitians, that culture, that resilience. They risked their lives helping others, being strong, and taking action. While I don't fear machetes and murdering soldiers today, I am very concerned and involved in stemming the ethnic violence, discrimination, and vehemence against women of color (WOC) that persists in the US today.

What my grandfather's stories taught me is that new life never emerges unless something is first "broken" while allowing the soul, spirit, or essence of the thing to remain and thrive. Don't be afraid of being broken, be afraid of not using that brokenness to create something better.

For him, life in Haiti was broken. His home, village, neighbors, and friends were broken. But so many of the people who weren't killed remained. Many of them went on to thrive after being broken. They became stronger, as is nature's way.

Trees and plants break through their seed or shell and then break through the soil or earth. They become what their DNA aided them to be—resilient. We, as human beings, burst out of our mothers, destined to become adults. Butterflies burst out of cocoons, chickens out of eggs. Runners burst through the tape stretched across the finish line. You get it. The world around us is a series of events that we break through—whether symbolically, intellectually, physically, emotionally, or wholly.

My ancestors broke through the chains and the political system, the times and the trauma that bound them. The more things change, the more they remain the same.

As adults we break through trauma, tragedy, and challenges before becoming who and what we were destined to be: change makers. As I interviewed each woman for this book so I could share their stories, I could hear the echoes of their ancestors, their culture, their challenges rising up in them as well. We survived. And now we thrive to become change makers of our generation.

Becoming Change Makers: The Exquisite Path to Leadership and Liberation for Women of Color is a transformational guide to helping you find your way through the unprecedented times we are living in. This book is an homage, an invitation, and a roadmap to this type of balanced leadership so that we can birth the country and conditions we ALL need to flourish, reach our potential, and transcend current circumstances and ways of being.

Following an honest exploration of the significant loss of life, trauma faced by communities of color, and ongoing microaggressions that have caused unnecessary suffering among our children, babies, and elders alike—this book offers a path for us to step into creating a new world.

Our goal in this book is to inspire WOC by helping us realize our own unique potential and leadership abilities. We are committed to fostering self-efficacy and igniting transformative change within ourselves and our communities. This guide is embraces all women, including those who are cisgender, transgender, lesbian, or nonbinary. Our aim is to inspire a ripple effect of self-actualization among us and the communities dear to us.

Introduction

Having weathered the storm so many have been subjected to day-after-day for years on end—it's time for us all to become change makers—to get out from under the pressure of what should be assumed and create something substantial, something ethical, something fantastically uncontainable that brings about our liberation.

This book will inspire you to find and amplify your voice, step into your place as a leader, and, most of all, unite with other change makers to usher forth a new dawn of hope and understanding in the world. *Becoming Change Makers* is here to show a way through these times of change and rebirth.

As a WOC and a mother, my children teach me much, including the depth of contradictions of adulthood and everyday life in the US. My daughter sometimes plays the backward day game, where she'll say something but mean the opposite.

Technically, National Backward Day falls on January 31 every year. It's an official day when adults and children do everything backward. Madness becomes sanity, and insanity becomes normal. I think it's an odd little holiday because it brings to light the ironic reality of life in the US. For example, materialism is most valued but love, relationships, and gratitude (the intangible) are what heals and fulfills.

We can often look to the opposite of the explicit value here and find the truth of what will help us truly live and thrive. In this twisted experience, there is a cost to everyone, but those who are explicitly oppressed suffer on multiple levels. For WOC, this cost is direct and holistic, and gets passed on through our bodies, minds, and generations.

If our daughters and sons, be it birthed, reared, or mentored, are to grow, heal, lead, and enjoy the lives they envision, we need to teach, coach, and mentor them. We need to raise them with the truths and realities of life, of their masculine and feminine energy, and of what a balance of the two look like.

WOC sit in a unique position in the US, one of insight and oppression, one that often experiences the brunt of racism, sexism, and other discriminatory stances. We do this while simultaneously, and too frequently, being expected to manage, organize, care for, and implement processes and practices that move a family, organization, corporation, or community forward.

Not all challenges come from racism and sexism. They can come from personal or professional trauma, mental illness, families, jobs, and a variety of obstacles as well. Challenges can come from learning to recognize, seize, and use our own power or growth in difficult environments.

Most of us, WOC, have had to directly confront this intersection of oppressive beams. However, through this compounded pain, many have risen to resist, heal, grow, achieve, and transcend. Pain can, and often does, breed empathy when healing is in the mix. Through empathy, a passion to change circumstances, and a love for community, WOC can be in a unique position to lead our communities, our states, and nations to liberation.

Some Life Experiences

"Hey nigger."

I froze.

I was 13 years old and walking home from school as usual. I had walked this path home from school for years, passing by my friend Jeremiah's house as always. Jeremiah was a White guy.

I thought he was a friend, or at least we were friendly. This particular day there was a group of boys there, all out on his porch.

Introduction

As I walked by one of them called out "nigger." Then another, until almost all of the group, many of them older boys, were calling out "nigger." I stopped in my tracks, frozen and unsure of what was going to happen next.

I looked over at them, saw Jeremiah, and thought, "Isn't he going to say something? Jeremiah, you know me. Say something." He didn't. He didn't yell nigger, but he didn't stand up for me either. Silence is also a statement.

I didn't know what to do. I didn't know if I should cuss at them or yell at them or if they would come after me or hurt me if I did respond.

It hurt for them to call me those names and it hurt just as much, or more, for Jeremiah to be silent. He just stood there doing nothing. Something inside me just withered and died. I never saw him the same again after that.

I was silent and tried to hold it together until I got home to my stepdad, a committed White, Polish, French-Canadian, US-born man, who could do nothing more than hold me as I cried.

My mom is an artistic and industrious Haitian and French woman. My biological father was a proud African American—a big, dark-skinned, Mississippi-born man. My parents were divorced when I was two and my mom married my stepdad, who raised me from the time I was three. My stepdad didn't quite know what to do in this environment either. He was trying to navigate this racial situation himself.

Here he was, a White man raising a little Black girl in this mostly White town. Add to that, his parents and my maternal grandma were racist. When I was born, my grandma didn't accept me because I was Black. It wasn't until I was an older child that she began to fully accept me.

Looking back at that experience on my way home from school, I can say it was the most memorable recollection I have of racism as a teenager. However, I can't say it was a total shock. After all, this small, rural town in Michigan where I was raised was less than an hour from the home of late KKK Grand Dragon Robert Miles. The racial tensions in my hometown were thick. I was one of a handful of people of color in the town, so I experienced direct racism on a regular basis.

It was my awareness of my grandfather's experiences, as well as the love from my parents' and the experiences from my own childhood, that sparked in me a desire to help heal the wounds of oppression I was witnessing around me.

I grew up, looked at what was happening in my community, and went to college, getting my PhD in counseling psychology with a specialization in consultation from Arizona State University.

I eventually became a community psychologist and founded BECOME, a nonprofit organization dedicated to collective healing and transformation toward thriving communities and a just world.

At BECOME, we use tools, including restorative facilitation, community organizing, culturally responsive research and evaluation, and community-driven strategy development and implementation, to transform our reality. As evaluators, organizers, and change agents, we use our tools to catalyze and shape desired change and move toward transformation, creating the conditions communities need to thrive. Our work has taken us on journeys that support parents leading change in their communities for their children, youth signing up voters, and community residents developing and employing strategies for neighborhood-level well-being.

Looking back at my childhood, I thought I was past the worst of life's challenges. Then, COVID-19 hit my immediate family hard in 2020.

Introduction

I began to work at home with a toddler and an infant, while my husband was laid off from his job. Our whole world changed. I was prepared to deal with helping people through this time based on things I'd learned on the way to my doctorate and beyond. Real life, including motherhood and marriage, wasn't among those classes.

As with many of the women who tell their stories here, it was in this "wilderness experience" that I was pushed by outward circumstances to confront my own unaddressed childhood trauma and racism, along with new tasks, work, and parenting habits. As a WOC, I also became acutely aware of the weight of the experience of tacit expectations of being daughters, partners, friends, etc.

This forced disruption of the pandemic caused a pause, not only in my internal world, but also in my team at BECOME. It caused us to reflect and review our past lessons learned. These reflections inspired this book.

Through our neighborhood organizing and evaluation work, WOC have risen as essential community leaders. We've also had the honor of working directly with organizations and programs dedicated to WOC. Research and evaluation findings from three of our evaluations, in particular, created the foundation for this guide. These programs support WOC leadership development in different ways, including community organizing, community-driven philanthropy, and nonprofit leadership: Cultivate is a program that strengthens the vital leadership of WOC community organizers and advocates; the Chicago Foundation for Women, which supports organizations serving women and girls, created a program to uplift and enhance donor diversity and community-driven philanthropy; and Public Allies, a national organization that trains and uplifts aspiring change makers into leaders for social justice, looked at their impact on women, particularly WOC.

Evaluation is a powerful tool that can be used to change lives. It's a systematic process of data collection, strategy, and engagement to learn and improve the effect or impact of programs, projects, policies, and initiatives. We applied Culturally Responsive Evaluation in each project, engaging WOC directly in the evaluation process in its development, analysis, and subsequent reporting/action planning.

The factual findings of our research, and the actual stories of a number of the women's lives who were a part of the evaluations, became not only the story of these programs and this book project, but also representative of many WOC's experience around the US.

We've tried to capture the mystery, the magic, the intensity, and the uniqueness of each participant's wisdom. We worked hard to tap into their vibe, their dream, their growth, and their experience as women, daughters, mothers, and leaders in their story as it relates to the topics and sections of this book.

Our goal is to present facts and awareness, along with a narrative to inspire readers and share our path and healing with you.

We hope you find something in these pages that not only touches the wounds of WOC but reveals the healing and wisdom that evolved from their healing journeys.

We hope we touch something within you that encourages you to deepen into your power. We hope you share and move on your path in new and more authentic ways or create new paths that work even better for you, your friends, your peers, and your communities.

The Design of the Book

This book is designed to walk women, particularly WOC, through a journey of compassionate and liberating leadership real-

Introduction

ization and a better understanding of our feminine energy and power.

The themes that emerged through our work across the projects mentioned previously serve as the sections of this book.

Each chapter is a conversation, a story, and an elaboration on aspects of the section's themes. There are snippets of women's leadership journeys in those specific areas. We also include recommendations for institutional leaders and environments where WOC work and share their "talents, time, and treasure."

NOTE: Kindly be aware that each chapter in this book comprises an introductory and interconnected narrative by yours truly, followed by the powerful stories of thirteen exceptional women who are part of the BECOME community. The interviews of these women were conducted in 2023. These women are either alumni of the projects BECOME evaluated or are a part of the BECOME team. This thoughtfully curated fusion seeks to engage and support readers on a unique and hopefully fulfilling journey.

* * *

Section 1 looks at healing and wholeness, what it is, what it means, and how to pursue it.

Section 2 dives into the importance of relationships.

Section 3 covers the concept of intersectionality, an essential topic when focusing on women of color.

Section 4 focuses on the responsible actualization and use of our power.

Each section includes details about each concept and ends with a chapter on applying lessons learned to organizations and neighborhood spaces.

Many of the women who participated in these evaluations have experienced personal trauma in various ways. They have, and still are, walking the path to healing, understanding the trauma that created both pain points and springboards for growth and compassion.

We understand that for many WOC, including some of our readers, unaddressed and unexpressed trauma continues to negatively impact their work and well-being as well as their ability to lead effectively. Thus, the women in our projects, and in this book, have stressed the need for healing and its process.

The necessity of healing goes beyond the themes of these evaluation projects to the collective wounds of low-income communities and communities of color in the US.

Psychology, science, and medical research have repeatedly proven that safe relationships are an essential key to healing physical, mental, and emotional traumas.[1]

The women in our studies spoke of relationships, trauma, and intersectionality as drivers of philanthropy, conduits to healing, scaffolding to professional development, and crucial to their communities' well-being.

The concept of intersectionality was introduced by legal scholar Kimberlé Crenshaw in 1989 and refers to the interconnected nature of various social categories, such as race, gender, class, sexuality, disability, and other identities.

Each category overlaps and intersects to create unique experiences of discrimination, learning, privilege, and oppression. For instance, WOC experience discrimination based not only on the color of our skin, but also on the fact that we're women. Add a difference in ability or sexual preference to that and you can see how people can simultaneously hold multiple social identities. These identities interact and influence each other, shaping a person's experiences and opportunities.

Introduction

Through healing, deepening relationships, and exploring our multifaceted selves, we can activate and shape our power and use it for the good of us, our families, and our communities. However, even power requires intentional exploration for us to tap into and use it responsibly.

By interviewing the WOC of the BECOME community, we gathered stories and insights that exemplify the topics in this book, including healing, trauma, self-love, power, the balance of masculine and feminine principles, culture, and the importance of connection, community, and communication.

Women interviewed for these stories elucidated examples of the themes that exemplified each section. These are true life stories and inspirational in and of themselves.

This book is also designed for both personal and collective reflection. There are reflection questions at the end of each chapter as well as a book club guide with all the chapters' reflection questions at the end of the book. We invite you to delve into reflection independently, as well as convene a group of friends, colleagues, family members, or the like to journey together.

Section One
Healing: Realizing its Magic

"Healing begins where the wound was made."

— Alice Walker

Whether we pray, meditate, attract, or manifest, we often associate healing with "magic" because of its ability to restore our health, wholeness, and well-being in a seemingly supernatural or extraordinary way. While healing can be explained through various scientific and medical means, the magic of healing goes beyond conventional explanations and our own understanding.

At its core, healing is about bringing balance and wholeness to a person's being. It is a process that acknowledges the interconnectedness of the body, mind, and spirit, recognizing that imbalances in one aspect of our lives can affect others. Healing often involves addressing the root causes of ailments, imbalances, or trauma rather than merely treating symptoms, focusing on achieving deep and lasting wellness.

The magic of healing lies in its ability to tap into the body's inherent wisdom and its capacity for self-repair. It's a reminder of the extraordinary resilience and regenerative power that exists within each of us. Whether it's through medical interventions that mend physical wounds, energy practices that restore energetic flow, or therapies that promote emotional release, healing empowers individuals to regain their vitality and reclaim their sense of wholeness.

Moreover, healing is not solely confined to the individual. It extends to the connections we have with others and the world around us. The magic of healing can be found in the compassionate presence of healers, therapists, or caregivers who provide support, understanding, and a nurturing environment for the healing process to unfold. Healing can also be facilitated through the power of community, as collective intentions, prayers, and loving energy can create an environment that fosters healing on a larger scale.

The magic of healing also encompasses the realms beyond the physical. It acknowledges that human beings are not just bodies, but also possess a spiritual essence that is intricately intertwined with their well-being. Healing can involve practices that reconnect people to their inner wisdom, divine presence, or higher purpose. It offers an opportunity for personal growth, self-discovery, and spiritual transformation.

In essence, the magic of healing lies in the potential for restoration, growth, and transcendence that it holds. It is a reminder of the remarkable capacity of the human spirit to heal, renew, and find harmony amid challenges. It invites us to embrace the miracles of our existence and tap into the innate power that resides within us.

Chapter 1
Trauma and Resilience

"It's only pain, it's only pain."

In 2012, I went on a spiritual pilgrimage to Nepal, where my group met the only woman shaman in the country at that time. One of the pieces of wisdom that came from being in her presence was this mantra: "It's only pain, it's only pain." I marveled at it and weighed it in my mind as we walked and throughout quiet moments on the trip. What did she mean, I wondered.

Pain often seems like it will kill us. It can feel overpowering, overwhelming, and relentless. It will either make or break us, depending on how we respond to it.

We all know what pain is—a mild to very unpleasant sensation that tells us something is unbalanced in our body, mind, or heart. Pain can be physical, mental, or deeply emotional. And it's different for everyone. We all feel pain, but we feel it differently depending on what it is and where it is.

Pain is not an equal-opportunity sensation. Cancer hurts differently than a migraine, which hurts differently than a sunburn, a limb amputation, loneliness, grief, or hunger. There's a reason for that—it depends on how our neurons are structured and what systems or pathways they use to alert our brain and body to what's happening. If you step barefoot on a Lego, for instance, you won't feel the pain in your hand.

If your child, spouse, or parent dies, the pain moves to your chest, heart, and upper body. Why?

The process is complex, involving dozens of hormones, chemicals, and various receptors for emotional pain. There is "good pain" and "bad pain" and science knows that how we sense, experience, and adapt to or tolerate pain is shaped by our genetics among other things.[1] Everyone (unless there is some sort of abnormality or psychopathy) will feel pain at some point in their life—both physical and emotional.

Trauma can contain various types of pain. It can also trigger the movement of pain through various parts our bodies and minds and over time and experience. Through the expression, understanding, and discharge of traumatic pain, our pain can be relieved, and we can see more clearly—and hopefully choose to evolve into our potential.

As Dr. Gabor Maté, a physician, trauma expert, author, and researcher, explains, "Trauma is not the bad things that happened *to you,* but what happens *inside you* as a result of what happened to you."[2]

For instance, one person can be in a car accident and be shaken up but not traumatized, while another may suffer post-traumatic stress disorder (PTSD) from the same accident. Some people go to war and come home, functioning fine, while others suffer PTSD and never function again. Such is the multifaceted face of trauma.

The experience of being victimized may cause a person to feel vulnerable or helpless. The victimization of people, through the media, culture, or familial reinforcement, may also change a person's world view, or self-perception, and causes psychological distress.[3]

As Dr. Maté explains, "It's a psychic wound that leaves a scar. It leaves an imprint in your nervous system, in your body, in your psyche, and then shows up in multiple ways that are not helpful to you later."[4]

Trauma is the physical, emotional, and mental impact of events on ourselves that remains long after physical scars have healed. It's also the shadows cast by the events of our lives—like a shadow, we can "see" it but not grasp it, or even realize what inside us is casting that shadow until we're able to throw a light on it.

You needn't have had a brutal childhood to have experienced trauma, but it's likely you have experienced trauma at some point in your life—nearly 100% likely if you're a WOC.[5]

A Chicago native, Cynthia Alfaro was the youngest of two daughters born to a Polish immigrant woman and a Mexican American man. Her culturally mixed heritage set the stage for her passion for diversity and equity in all arenas she worked.

It was in education and athletics that Cynthia started studying leadership and life success factors that would later reap even more benefits as an adult. Even as a child, she was resilient, independent, and ambitious. She attended the well-known Whitney Young Magnet High School and was once nationally ranked in competitive tennis. "Both my elementary and high school exposed me to the places where I wanted to be and helped me get there," she said.

With her upbringing and educational resources, Cynthia never expected to confront the trauma she experienced as an adult:

> Domestic violence was a topic that was foreign to me. We heard about it in some classes I took. I remembered the auditorium talks and some speaker saying, "One out of three of us will experience it…" but it was so far from my own awareness that when I actually found myself in this situation as an adult, I was not only

surprised, but stunned. I didn't realize until then that "I" was "the one" in those "one in three."

Many women don't realize they are or have been traumatized. Until they have something to compare their life with, their daily or past trauma seems normal to them. Some people may have limited knowledge or understanding of what constitutes trauma. They may not be familiar with the symptoms, effects, or different types of traumas. As Cynthia recalled:

> My domestic violence situation was a relationship that started at the church, which I also feel contributed to part of the difficulty of removing the layers and pulling away from it. I had some beliefs that weren't helping me leave, that were wrapped up in the religion of things. Eventually, I was able to pull out.
>
> There is a particular instance that stands out. I was held captive in my kitchen for hours. Who knows for what. There was never really a rhyme or reason as to how something starts.
>
> My first daughter was crying in the other room, and I couldn't go get her because I was being threatened. I was told that if I were to leave or try to get out, the police would have to come. It wasn't until later in life that I realized that I was living around a certain level of trauma.
>
> I was just trying to make it through. I didn't acknowledge or process it or think about it in those terms. I don't think that's unusual. A lot of people still live with those traumas and it's like, that's just how it is.

Cynthia wasn't alone in her confusion. In certain situations, trauma can become normalized or downplayed. Those who experience it might believe that what they went through is a common part of life or that others experience similar things. They may believe that even though things are painful, and they feel threatened and dehumanized, it's normal. They may not realize that their experiences are significant and have had (or will have) a lasting impact. Cynthia explains:

> My family would say things like, "Oh, the postpartum was so rough on you." In the meantime, I was thinking, "Let me tell you. It wasn't just that. I was also being intimidated in my own house."

> There were horrible situations. I remember thinking that this was not life. I was constantly having to walk on eggshells, and it got to a point where my emotions were off their rocker. I was so desperate that I would talk to strangers on the street in tears, just asking for guidance, help, or something like that. It was a really rough time.

> Eventually, I left. The intimidation was more intense than a beating. It was enough for me to be like, "Okay, that's it." I left and stayed with a friend.

> I tried making the relationship work again for a little bit because this was the father of my kids, and we were going to counseling and we had the church connection and all this other stuff. Redemption and forgiveness and blah, blah, blah.

> Then, baby number two came. I wanted it to happen. I don't think there's a person who doesn't want it to happen—the two-parent household—especially since I didn't have my dad. I was like, "No. This can't happen for me, either." There was a lot of that.

Feelings of shame, guilt, or self-blame can make it difficult for us to recognize our experiences, whether severe or not, as trauma. We may internalize societal or cultural narratives that place blame on the victim or imply that they somehow caused or deserved the traumatic events. This can create barriers to recognizing traumatization.

At a time when we need people the most, trauma can negatively impact our relationships with others. If we have no, or few friends, our trauma contributes to difficulties in forming and maintaining healthy connections. We may have trust issues, both at work and at home. We'll often experience social withdrawal or difficulties with intimacy and closeness, as Cynthia expounds:

> After I moved out and depleted my entire 401(k), I found myself trapped in a web of manipulation and control. The support I needed to catch my breath was nowhere to be found. Believe me, everyone deserves a momentary respite. It wasn't until my youngest turned three and a half that I finally had a chance to take a break and let me tell you, the mental toll was staggering.
>
> I started having panic attacks. The stress started as a little jump in my eyes as I would be driving with my girls. There was never a time when I was without my girls.
>
> I was not able to go places with friends that I had because they didn't have kids yet. I was excluded from things. I couldn't go anywhere without my kids. There are a lot of places where kids aren't welcome or it's not conducive for them. The jump in my eye was stress starting and it eventually got to be full-on panic attacks.
>
> I had two panic attacks that let me know that I had to leave immediately. It was the one moment in my life when it was such a big idea. I couldn't even speak about it because I couldn't even fathom how after 14 years, how do I leave, not only with myself but with two little kids.
>
> I'm in debt. My rent hasn't been paid in about four months. I can't even afford chicken nuggets. How do you expect me to leave, even though I need to? I was not eating; I was not sleeping. I had to take pills to go to sleep, but those would make me feel groggy. It was a terrible time.

I talked with some doctors and started to go to therapy. What I did know was that I did not want this to sideline me for the next decade. I immediately jumped into therapy and was like, "Here's our goal. I need to be functioning. I need to be well. I need to make it through this. I have these two little girls that need to survive and it's all on me." I was doing my work to heal at a rapid pace so I didn't stay in this ditch. It's so easy to stay in the ditch.

Eventually, once the panic attacks happened and I had to leave. I decided to come back home. My friends from New York gave me money so I could find an apartment. My best friend let me stay with her at first. People gave me kind of a communal hug. One of my friends from Pepsi got me a job.

There was so much shame involved with this, so much guilt involved in this. Once I settled into it, I thought, "This is part of your story." The story is really not for me. It's for everybody else. It's to be shared. Nobody would guess, nobody would think, "Not Cynthia. Not the high achiever. Not the honor roll high school vice president, nationally ranked tennis player." But yes. It's Cynthia.

I still have to manage my anxiety, but I'm so much better now. My sleep is so much better now. It took real separation. Society will tell you that it (life) needs to look like this, it needs to look like that.

Even my closest friends have given me pushback about the thick wall that I've put between my girls' father and our lives right now. I said, "Well, I am still trying to save myself here."

I feel like society puts way too much on our shoulders as mothers to be the ones to hold it all. I refuse to hold it all. I can't hold somebody else's toxic language and disrespect in order for my kids to communicate with them. I'm not doing that. I am traumatized. I am injured. I am impacted, so I need to get healthy because they rely on me.

It took years of feeling bad and feeling guilty for that. Now that I'm on the other side, it's the lesser of two evils. I don't wish it to be like this at all. But at the same time, I don't need to hold on to somebody else's decisions like it's my fault.

Now, I know after years of therapy that I'm a historical people pleaser to the point where I overextend myself and ignore my boundaries to make something work. At the same time, I end up dishonoring myself.

Now I know this. I can change things and figure out where in my past I learned these behaviors. If it wasn't for the trauma and the challenges and getting into therapy, I wouldn't have grown. I wouldn't have learned all the things I did.

Our ability to regulate our emotions—which makes us moody, irritable, angry, or emotionally numb—is impacted by trauma. We may have extreme mood swings and feel overwhelmed by the simplest of emotions. All that *feels* normal because at the time, it's *our normal.*

Our self-esteem, self-worth, and sense of identity often plummet. This leads to feelings of shame, self-blame, or distorted self-perception, and a lifetime of healing. Numbness or emotional detachment can be a common response to traumatic experiences, or a defense mechanism—that allows us to disconnect from over-whelming emotions and protect ourselves from further psychological harm. This response, known as dissociation, is the mind's way of creating a temporary barrier against the intense emotions associated with trauma.

Our childhood and our biology create the foundation for how we handle trauma, be it healthy or unhealthy. Looking back at her childhood, Cynthia recalls such a layered life:

I remember playing with roaches in my Barbie truck. It sounds gross, but it was what it was. I didn't know any better at the time.

Looking back on my life and the things that happened to people around me at the time, I realize now, oh, this person committed suicide, that person overdosed.

There's no awareness or sense of trauma over those events because it was just how life all around me was. It was "my normal." No one really talked about it one way or another. Like the roaches, it was what I grew up with.

Both my elementary and high school exposed me to the places where I wanted to be and helped me get there. Other than not having my dad around, nothing injured me then.

What happened to me is not any different than what was happening to many people at the time and still happens to many people. Did it feel traumatic? I don't know. It was what I was used to. I didn't know anything else.

"Nothing injured me." For many women, nothing injuring us is seen as a strength, a skill, proof of our toughness and our resilience. "Nothing injuring us," or nothing triggering strong emotions, can be both a trauma response, as well as a sign of resilience, depending on the context and individual experiences.

Adverse Childhood Experiences

Trauma often begins with adverse childhood experiences (ACEs). These are psychologically harmful events or circumstances that occur during childhood. These events have the potential to negatively impact a child's development and well-being. ACEs range from physical, sexual, and emotional abuse, to neglect, poverty, racism, losing a parent to death, divorce, or mental illness, and dysfunctional parenting.[6]

Research has found that ACEs are common: 62% of US adults surveyed reported experiencing at least one adversity during childhood. ACEs are even higher for socioeconomically and racially diverse populations, with nearly 70% reporting at least one ACE.[7]

Psychologists recognize that exposure to ACEs can significantly impact a child's development and functioning, self-concept, beliefs about the world, ability to form healthy relationships, and control or regulate their overall emotions.

ACEs have been linked to increased risk for mental health disorders like depression, anxiety, post-traumatic stress disorder, substance abuse, and a higher likelihood of engaging in risky behaviors or having difficulties in school.

Even more disturbing, especially for WOC, is the fact that unaddressed trauma, including ACEs, impact our ability to lead teams and to be managers, coaches, mentors, or parents.

Unaddressed or unresolved trauma can keep us from being the most effective participants in or able to fully contribute to our communities and to be happy and healthy. We don't even realize our past is holding us back until suddenly, we do. It might be a new job, a relationship, or hearing a talk about someone else's life that flips the switch inside us that triggers our awareness.

Trauma exists in the depths of our psyche, often hidden from conscious awareness—but emerging in nightmares, panic attacks, anxiety, or destructive habits. Traumatic experiences and their associated emotions, memories, and beliefs can become repressed or dissociated for years. They rest in the corners of our minds until triggered by our inner or outer environment—our personal growth, having children of our own, changing jobs, being placed in a leadership position, or experiencing personal or professional growth or demands on us.

The shadow self, or sub- and unconscious thoughts and feelings, within us is shaped by trauma and can influence our behavior and relationships in profound ways. We may exhibit patterns of avoidance, hypervigilance, or aggression as defense mechanisms, resulting from the shadow's impact on our thoughts, emotions, and worldview. This shadow self can also affect our ability to trust, form intimate connections, or navigate interpersonal dynamics—causing us to "stall out" in relationships, or at work.

Addressing the trauma and healing the shadow self involves acknowledging, embracing, and integrating the fragmented aspects of ourselves. This is part of the pathway of resilience.

Understanding trauma as a shadow self helps illustrate the profound impact it can have on our psyche and overall well-being. By acknowledging and addressing this shadow self, we can embark on a healing journey to reclaim our sense of self, heal from the wounds of the past, and move towards a brighter, more integrated future.

Fortunately, what happens to us does not define or dictate who we are or who we can BECOME.

Resilience

When our awareness of our trauma (past or current) begins to emerge, so does a new consciousness about our *resilience*, or our ability to bounce back, adapt, and recover in the face of adversity, challenges, or significant life stressors. Resilience is the capacity to withstand and navigate through difficult situations, setbacks, or traumatic experiences. We often develop resilience before we become aware of our trauma—as Cynthia did:

> I grew up in Chicago in an immigrant lifestyle—probably the most violent neighborhood in Chicago at the time. None of my friends would visit me because they didn't feel safe there.
>
> The immigrant lifestyle is one of a lot of people coming from your country, living with you until they can get their own lives

set up. Life at my grandmother's was busy. That was just what it was like growing up. I became really self-determined. My mom would say that I put myself to sleep every night. I brushed my teeth. I was on my own and getting myself together at a very early age, which I still find very weird, but it is what it is.

Growing up was tough at times and uncomfortable. But I wouldn't have changed it because it taught me so much. If we are not uncomfortable, we don't seek change. So the pain or trauma you're experiencing blesses you in that it pushes you to grow in ways you'd never think about unless you were in pain.

Growth is all about being able to step outside of your comfort zone and taking the uneasiness that comes at first. You're changing your emotional and mental environment and leaving what you know and exchanging it for something you haven't experienced before. It can be hard—harder than staying with the abuse.

Following a trauma or injury, our instinct is to bury those feelings and encounters deep within ourselves, and forge ahead. We convince ourselves that we are resilient, dismissing the anger, frustration, and injustices festering inside us. However, this does not truly cultivate resilience; instead, it often amplifies the trauma. To truly become resilient, we must acknowledge, confront, and grapple with our anger, frustration, and emotions.

Resilience refers to our ability to adapt and recover from adversity. We may initially experience numbness or emotional detachment but then gradually regain our emotional responsiveness and ability to cope with the trauma. Over time, we develop healthy coping mechanisms, seek support, and engage in healing processes. These are all signs of resilience—the ability to skillfully manage stress and find healthy ways to navigate through life's challenges.

Trauma and Resilience

Resilience is not about being able to numb, avoid, or deny difficult situations, but rather about our ability to face trauma and challenges head-on. It involves utilizing personal strengths, coping strategies, and support systems to maintain a sense of stability, hope, and optimism.

Resilience is a complex trait, created when various factors, including personal characteristics, coping strategies, support systems, and environmental factors come together to help the person cope and survive. It always results from learning to cope with trauma—both as a child and an adult.

People often say things like, "My childhood trauma made me resilient." That's a powerful statement, but not quite accurate. Trauma merely kicks open the door to the opportunity to feel and become more resilient. Resilience doesn't heal trauma. It just gives us the space and time to begin the healing process. It's the internal mother who hugs and holds us as we cry, and whispers, "It's gonna be okay," while the rest of us figures out how to make that happen. It requires some practice and self-awareness to become a person who can adapt, bounce back, and recover from difficult or challenging situations, adversity, or trauma.

Resilience gives us a sense of strength and well-being during and after adverse or traumatic events. It holds the capacity to withstand and navigate through additional adversity, trauma, or challenges while maintaining mental, emotional, and physical well-being.

Resilience when combined with love or compassion can spark movement within us to try to help others who have experienced similar situations, like Cynthia:

> Race was difficult for me. I didn't speak Spanish. I didn't feel
> Mexican enough to others. As half Polish, half Mexican, I wasn't
> full White either. I came from a family of immigrants and a
> mixed cultural background but ended up connecting mostly

with the African American community. I always say my story is like *West Side Story*, the Chicago remix.

Most of my schools at the time were majority Black. I loved that I got to meet people from all around the city and to feel included in many places. That network of inclusion still means a lot to me.

Outside the home, I was having this rich, multicultural experience. But, sometimes at family functions, I heard racial slurs that didn't sit well with me. I was interrupting conversations at a very young age to say, "I don't think that's right."

Feeling isolated and feeling excluded a lot growing up really helped me to know how exclusion and inclusion look and feel innate. That innate awareness of inclusion and exclusion is so basic that most people miss it. It comes from being immersed in the culture at the survival level as a child.

I learned advocacy at the same time in the same way. Whether I heard racist stuff or something was happening to my friends while we were at a store I was observing and knowing what justice and injustice looked like. I was in touch with an inner wisdom that said, "This is right. This is not right." I paid attention to that voice and never let anyone or anything silence it.

Cynthia went on to earn an master's in finance and a master's in human resources from the University of Illinois Urbana-Champaign. Between undergrad and grad school, she completed a national volunteerism assignment with Public Allies Chicago, an AmeriCorps program, where she managed programs for community entrepreneurship, parent enrichment, and literacy.

Cynthia began working for PepsiCo in human resources in 2004 and later switched sectors and moved to specialize in training and development for the New York City Department of Education Alternative Programs in 2009.

Continuing her work in education, she took a school administrator position for a progressive dual language school in Manhattan and then moved back to Chicago where she supported the Chicago Public Schools in finance and business operations.

As a culmination of all her skills and talents, Cynthia recently finished a remarkable tenure as chief operating officer at My Block My Hood My City where she elevated the cause of the social justice organization. She is currently a coach and consultant for people and organizations that want to thrive and elevate their cause. She specializes in strategic planning, leadership development, operational efficiency, and culture for optimal performance.

In 2013, Cynthia started a blog called Moms Winning. She was in the midst of a hard life trial and decided to use her pain as a platform for others, by focusing on the "wins" of everyday life as a mother, whether big or small and allowing gratitude to push moms into a better way of living.

Resilience is an admirable trait, one that WOC have historically shown to be part of our identity. However, resilience does not mean being unaffected by traumatic experiences or simply "getting over" them or stuffing down our emotions about our trauma and challenges.

Resilience is a process that may look different for each person because it develops and becomes strengthened over time through intentional effort and practice.

Building resilience does not mean that a person won't experience challenges or setbacks. They will. But having good resilience skills equips us with the tools and mindset to navigate and bounce back from those difficulties.

We are the only ones who can ignite our power, pick ourselves up, and step on that path to healing. And while expressing emotions is critical, it doesn't mean allowing ourselves to be overwhelmed by them or to act impulsively on them. It's a balance between acknowledging and regulating our emotions, so they do not become overwhelming or detrimental to our well-being, and expressing our feelings appropriately.

Becoming and being resilient means acknowledging, understanding, and expressing our emotions—most notably those emotions that arise from trauma, abuse, and challenges—not hiding from them, or stuffing them down.

Because resilience is not a fixed trait, but a dynamic process that can be developed and nurtured over time, we can create it, strengthen it, and teach it. We do this through:

- **Relationships:** When we have or create positive relationships with family members, friends, mentors, or supportive communities, we create a crucial foundation for resilience. Caring and reliable people who offer emotional support, guidance, and encouragement can help us build resilience.
- **Healing and wholeness:** Learning and practicing effective coping strategies, including communication skills, can enhance our resilience. By developing healthy problem-solving skills, emotion regulation techniques, stress management strategies, and positive self-care practices we step on the path and begin our journey of healing.
- **Self-love:** Fostering a positive sense of self-worth and self-belief or "self-love" also contributes to our resilience. By recognizing our strengths, setting achievable goals, and celebrating our successes we can enhance our ability to address, navigate, and learn from our challenges and setbacks.

Even as we work to heal, to develop our resilience, and to move forward, we will still experience trauma's impact. Building resilience is a lifetime goal, not a one-time event.

BECOME exists because, at that intersection of hurt and our emotional responses, our power as people, especially WOC, comes together to make us stronger, truly resilient, and able to heal and positively impact our communities and the world. Through our pain, we can hone our purpose and create a more just and loving society.

Leadership and the Importance of Healing Trauma

What Cynthia learned was how the experiences of trauma and healing revolve around our heart—the things and people we love, and the things and people that love (or don't love) us back. She learned another, even more, invaluable lesson: healing is a path to leadership. And leadership is the path to reclaiming our lives and helping others reclaim theirs.

As leaders, we must heal or at least be working on our own trauma healing before we can lead others. Yes. You read that right. You cannot lead well or become a balanced leader until you have begun to address and heal your own trauma.

Not addressing and healing your trauma will not only impact your leadership style, your skills, and your ability to communicate with your team, your employees, your neighbors, and your business, it will retraumatize you as you try to work out the trauma in your professional and lived environment.[8]

In an article for *Forbes*, Kelly Campbell, a trauma-informed leadership coach, wrote, "Since people don't operate in silos, untreated trauma can hinder one's journey to cultivating relationships, building trust, and considering others in all decision-making processes."[9]

The toxic boss, the bullying coworker, the micromanaging manager—all have possibly suffered childhood trauma, Campbell says. The toxic and unhelpful, maladaptive behaviors we learned as children no longer serve us well as adults, and it shows when we move into a leadership position.

Unhealed leaders are visible in the way they handle or fail to handle challenges, obstacles, and communication. Healing leaders are better able to model healthy behavior, boundaries, compassion, and self-awareness, which in turn creates a safer work environment.

We cannot take or lead anyone past the point where we ourselves have been. Trying to do so will frustrate not only you, but also the person or people you're attempting to lead.

Trauma doesn't prevent us from *becoming leaders.* It just delays or prevents us from reaching our leadership potential. Healing is not a destination, but a journey. Healing our trauma is an important path to healthy leadership.

For leaders to lead others on a healing journey, they must be on a healing journey themselves.

Saying, "That's in my past. I'm fine. I don't want to go back there. I've got this. It didn't affect me that much," and all the other things we say to justify not dealing with our trauma is us lying to ourselves.

That denial of our past also hurts us, marginalizes us, and retraumatizes us. All the women interviewed for this book have experienced at least one ACE, and most have had several.

They have made amazing strides and overcome profound pain or trauma, and they are still healing while leading and demonstrating remarkable leadership skills as they do so. Healing oneself is not selfish.

Admitting to and sharing stories of your own journey, your own traumas and your own struggles is courageous and appropriate. Healing our past strengthens our ability to listen and care for others and lead well and better. The women in this book who share their stories reported a sense of relief and pride in sharing their pain, as well as their healing path or purpose-filled journey. They all became healthier and more powerful from what they experienced and overcame. You're not alone in your trauma, or in your healing.

Healing requires shining a light on the shadows and bringing them into conscious awareness. Through therapy, self-reflection, and support, we can explore our trauma, process the emotions associated with it, and work toward integrating the shadow self with our overall identity. This process can lead to greater self-understanding, resilience, and a sense of wholeness.

If you truly want to lead, your own healing is not an option, but a necessity. If you haven't addressed your own issues around trust, vulnerability, and trauma, then it's time to start. Healing doesn't mean you'll be perfect. You'll make mistakes. You'll offend or frustrate. You'll learn. You'll get better each step of the way. You have to begin your healing journey by choosing it, and stepping out on the path to knowledge, awareness, truth, and actualization of our inherent wholeness. Going on the journey is the goal.

Chapter 1: Trauma and Resilience

1. Reflecting on your journey, how have you turned challenges into opportunities for growth?
2. How have your experiences shaped your story and inspired others?

Cynthia Alfaro

Cynthia Alfaro (she/her), a Chicago native, is the youngest daughter of a Polish immigrant mother and a Mexican American father. Her multicultural background fueled her drive for diversity and equity in all fields. While studying leadership and success factors in education and athletics, Cynthia attended Whitney

Young Magnet High School and achieved national rankings in competitive tennis.

She earned a master's in finance and a master's in human resources from the University of Illinois Urbana-Champaign.

Between undergrad and grad school, she completed a national volunteerism assignment with Public Allies Chicago, an AmeriCorps program, where she managed programs for community entrepreneurship, parent enrichment, and literacy.

Cynthia's experience spans human resources at PepsiCo, the New York City Department of Education, training and school administration, finance, and business operations with Chicago Public Schools. As chief operating officer of My Block My Hood My City, she advanced the organization's social justice cause. Cynthia now coaches and consults on strategy, leadership, efficiency, and culture for top performance.

In 2013, during a hard life trial, Cynthia started Moms Winning to focus on the "wins" of motherhood. She believes that gratitude can push moms into a better way of living. Cynthia uses her training background to provide community workshops and advice on time management and goal setting for mothers.

Dedicated to service, Cynthia enjoys life with her two daughters and loves maintaining a healthy lifestyle through proper nutrition and exercise while helping others do the same.

Chapter 2
The Heart and Healing

As a child, I watched my father, a Black-presenting Puerto Rican with a thick Spanish accent, experience trial after trial while trying to find steady work to feed our family.

He couldn't find work in Yonkers, New York, where I was born. He also couldn't maintain a job when he did find one. Like many immigrants of color, my parents suffered constant indignities. I witnessed many of these indignities. I suffered traumatic stress from seeing them, and knowing I too was hated and thought less of for no reason other than I was a child of color born to immigrant parents of color, I was pained.

My heart ached watching how the world impacted my parents' lives and as a result, my life as well. Even as a child, I vowed to create better experiences for my family and other people of color in the world when I grew up.

— Michelle Morales

Michelle Morales is president of the Woods Fund Chicago. Before assuming this position, she played a vital role in leading the Illinois chapter of the Mikva Challenge. Recognized as a distinguished organization focusing on youth development civics, the Mikva Challenge creates an environment for young individuals to actively participate and emerge as leaders.

With 16 years of experience as a community organizer in Chicago's Puerto Rican community, Michelle tirelessly championed community development, education justice, and economic equity, all while advocating for Puerto Rico's independence. She valiantly opposed the swift gentrification of the Humboldt Park neighborhood in Chicago and played a pivotal role in coordinating an international campaign, successfully securing the release of 14 Puerto Rican political prisoners incarcerated in US prisons.

Despite the inherent pain that comes with heartache, it serves a profound purpose. It reminds us of our vitality and our capacity to experience emotions and, above all, it assures us that pain is fleeting and healing is possible. Michelle's journey is a testament to this truth. The unrelenting indignities she encountered in her formative years became defining moments that not only helped her discover her life's purpose, but also fueled her drive to achieve success.

Heartache encompasses the profound emotional anguish resulting from significant loss or disappointment, whether in matters of love and relationships or the erosion of cultural identity and community. The process of healing the heart entails not only tending to and mending the wounds and traumas that impact our emotional well-being, but also reclaiming our ability to foster meaningful connections with others and ourselves.

Recognizing the pain we carry within us presents its own set of challenges. It often requires us to delve deep into difficult emotions, memories, and beliefs. Sometimes, this even means reliving those painful experiences. However, by acknowledging and giving validity to our emotions, we embark on a transformative journey of processing and healing from our emotional wounds.

The Heart and Healing

For many WOC, the trauma of racism, poverty, and other ACEs has left an indelible mark on our hearts, causing us pain in countless ways. Some of us have suffered the loss of our parents or endured a myriad of challenging events. In Michelle's case, heartache arrived on multiple fronts, including the loss of her Puerto Rican heritage and a profound awareness of being disconnected from her cultural roots.

At BECOME, we meet and engage with many WOC and other people of color who are experiencing heartache, pain, and recovery. Many are well along the path to healing. Others are just starting out on their journey. But the connection is that they all have something to share about their process.

Socioeconomic struggles and racism contribute to heartache, which can stem from various sources such as relationship endings, the passing of a loved one, unreciprocated affection, or any circumstance that triggers emotional distress or sadness. This encompassing pain permeates our lives, reminding us of the complexity of human experiences and the profound impact they have on our well-being.

Coping with one's own heartache can be challenging, but coping with the heartache of family and friends can change your life—as it did with Michelle:

> My mother was Puerto Rican and a homemaker for her entire life. She raised three children, and like my father, she was proud of her heritage, but I don't think either of them understood what it meant to teach us what it meant to be Puerto Rican, in terms of history or culture.
>
> There was a cognitive dissonance there—we really weren't taught why we should be proud to be Puerto Ricans, or exactly what it meant to be Puerto Rican. We didn't learn anything about our culture or history, but we observed and endured the

abuse and discrimination that came along with being this thing my parents were so proud of.

My father's frequent work changes eventually led to his joining the military after my brother was born, around the time I was two.

We became a military family and led a transient, military-type lifestyle colored with distrust and anger. We were raised all over the place on military bases where there were no Puerto Ricans except for those who were living on the military base.

My siblings—a brother and a sister—and I grew up knowing a few other Puerto Ricans, but we were often the only Puerto Ricans and the only Latinos, period, in our school.

Culturally, there were things that we would pick up when we would visit our family in New York, but there was nothing structured around a cultural education. There wasn't even Puerto Rican music played in the house. I think my parents just thought we would pick up Puerto Rican culture through osmosis.

We weren't taken to Puerto Rico as children, and the last time my parents went back was for their honeymoon 48 years ago. They've never expressed the desire to go back since then.

I was the first one, at 19, to go back to the Island. I've been back about five times. My husband and my son have gone twice. It was a thing for me to make sure that our child experienced Puerto Rico and visited the island as a child. We're trying to figure out going back now that he's 18.

I became the first and only family member to attend college, attain graduate degrees, and become an organizational leader.

The way I see it is I came from a legacy of people who have fought for their freedom and to ensure that their culture and the vibrancy of Puerto Rico will not be diminished. Being Puerto Rican means being part of a people who have historically resisted and being part of a legacy of a people who are probably too resilient.

We're so resilient that sometimes the government doesn't take care of us the way they should. We have a legacy as people who are ridiculously creative, and proud of it.

I was fortunate to have carved out a path to equity in a northwest-side neighborhood in Chicago called Humboldt Park. Humboldt Park used to be a predominantly Puerto Rican neighborhood, which did two things—it allowed me to identify with and take pride in my Puerto Rican heritage and to flourish among my tribe and culture.

If we don't intentionally reconnect with our inherent wholeness, the results can perpetuate oppression, abuse, neglect, and dehumanization.

Others will feel the effects of past slights and abuses through our actions, many times inadvertently because we subconsciously mimic our role models and what we experienced growing up.

Our brains are hardwired to create actions and experiences based on our childhood. We can't be what we don't know or haven't experienced growing up. We have to not only heal from the abuses we've suffered, but also learn to identify them in ourselves and break the cycle.

This path leads to our own liberation from past traumas, psychological oppression, and negative self-talk. It leads to our bigness, our beauty, and our light. Michelle shares:

> I've dedicated myself to creating a just society for years now, but I recently realized I was perpetuating micro-injustices at work. Most of my supervisors were cisgender men who controlled and dictated almost everything, from the tasks themselves to who got to carry them out.

I am ashamed to say I learned from those controlling leaders who were my only leader role models. Seeing their success, I thought I had to control and protect my vision too. But my team called me out on it last year, and I finally realized that controlling everything puts your vision at risk.

They shared that I had a tendency to micromanage people. I didn't see it that way. I thought I was being helpful by leaning in. I thought that by taking things off of people's plates or volunteering to do things for them, I was being helpful. They saw my actions as distrusting them. They told me, "You don't trust us to do this. You are dictating how things should get done." I would delegate but then I would say, "I would like it this way." Instead of just saying, "Here's the task. Do you have any questions?" At no point did I think any of those things were controlling. It's stunning how deep-seated these beliefs and our conditioning can go.

Many of us striving for social justice have experienced or witnessed grave injustices, resulting in lingering wounds and scars. These harms go beyond what we realize, violating our dignity and compromising our psychology. To effectively advocate and lead, healing is essential on our liberated journey. It's important to acknowledge the impacts of hierarchical leadership, personal traumas, and microaggressions, as they manifest in our bodies and minds.

Healing is not only crucial for our own well-being but also for advocating for social justice causes. Michelle has shown that it's possible to delve into intersectionality (i.e., the intersection of different cultural identities), process feelings, and contribute to others' healing journeys. However, advocating for social justice can be emotionally challenging if we haven't healed our own hearts, particularly when engaging with issues of abuse. Recognizing the intersectionality of different oppressions and how it shows up in us is vital in the pursuit of social justice.

By embarking on the healing journey, we can uplift ourselves and become our best selves as well as inspiring others to do the same. Through this restorative path are mountains of joyous and wonderous explorations and realizations of the exquisite truth of who we are and the power that lies within and around us.

The Process of Healing

Healing is a process of reconnecting with one's higher self. It starts with reflection and awareness, exploring thoughts, emotions, and experiences to align with our authentic nature.

Tapping into our higher self allows us to access inner guidance and intuition about our purpose and life path. Trusting this wisdom enables us to make decisions that align with our values and desires. This connection also provides purpose, direction, and clarity throughout our healing journey.

As we explore more about ourselves, we find that we have to let go of limiting beliefs, patterns, and habits that no longer serve us. By freeing ourselves from old ways of thinking we open ourselves to new experiences, allowing us to reach our full potential.

Healing requires more than just managing pain and addressing trauma. Cultivating love and compassion for ourselves and others is also key. Our higher self is rooted in love and compassion. Extending these to those around us supports interconnectedness and empathy, which fosters healing on a collective level. By reconnecting with our loving self and other aspects of ourselves, we can offer ourselves forgiveness, acceptance, and kindness—essential ingredients for healing.

One of the best ways to heal is to go within. It's like taking a journey to find your very own treasure. Like an archeologist who picks up a shovel and digs, we too must use our inner tools to dig deep within. One might uncover rocks that seem like burdens, or brush away layers of dirt to reveal friendships or experiences we have been taking for granted. But along the way, you might unearth a sense of joy, purpose, or fulfillment—the very treasure you have been searching for all this time. With each journey within ourselves, we can discover, create and align with our core values and ultimately, lead a more fulfilling life.

This conscious attention to our core values forces us to consider living with integrity, making choices, and taking actions that resonate with our authentic selves, rather than seeking external validation or conforming to societal expectations.

When we know and honor our core values, we create a sense of congruence and harmony within ourselves. This congruence and awareness contribute to our healing and personal growth.

Healing, or reconnecting with the higher self, is deeply personal and transformative. When we heal or reconnect, we access our inner wisdom, find inner peace, and live a more authentic and fulfilling life.

The concept of a higher self can vary among different spiritual, religious, or philosophical traditions. Each person's experience and understanding of the higher self can be unique and very personal. I believe that the process of connecting with this higher self is the essence of healing.

This process also includes connecting with others authentically. For someone seeking to recover from trauma, building a trusting and healthy connection with another person is one of the most beneficial things we can do. Having someone to share thoughts and feelings with, and to process the emotions and thoughts associated with traumatic experiences, can be truly transformative.

It's a journey, and not always the one we anticipate when we begin. The twists and turns that life takes us on are nothing like we imagine growing up. There is no clear path, and all is not as it appears. Michelle's journey didn't end with the cultural and emotional heartache she experienced. That was just the beginning.

The Heart and Healing

She experienced just how much a person can be shaped by pain and heartache when she received a cancer diagnosis:

> I had no idea what kind of pain, or healing, I would go through with cancer. I just knew I was about to begin an incredible journey and I had absolutely no idea what to expect along the way.
>
> I know now that I never gave myself that type of space before. I was always moving and on the go. "Being on the go" made me feel good. It made me feel productive. It made me feel successful. But I never gave myself the downtime or the quiet time to reflect internally. I did that for those six weeks during recovery, and that started the process—which is ongoing now—of more spiritual and emotional healing.

At first glance, many of us assume that all healing is physical—as in Michelle pinpointing her journey beginning with her double mastectomy. It took time for her to stop and relax enough for the spiritual and emotional healing to get her attention on all levels: spiritual, emotional, and physical.

Just as a community can be different, healing itself can have many definitions. T. R. Egnew argues that healing is not simply the absence of disease or the relief of symptoms, but rather that it's a transformational process that involves transcending suffering.[1] Egnew suggests that healing involves the integration of the physical, emotional, and spiritual dimensions of a person's life.

For instance, if you want to build muscle, you must first break down the existing muscle in a controlled way that allows or forces the muscle to heal, to rebuild itself. Healing involves pain, effort, and time. And it also teaches us about discipline, pain, goal setting, and ourselves in the process. The breaking down and rebuilding process is also a type of healing.

Healing is also a catharsis that can include reconciling, recognizing, and realizing. In healing, when we tap into our higher self, we see ourselves with loving and unified eyes. We're now able to see a deeper truth and live into that truth. We move away from the distortions of this reality into clarity, inspiration, and love.

Healing is holistic. It requires the mind, body, and spirit to tap into the wholeness that exists under our misguided and corrupted notions of self and life. We're not like a car or an appliance in which we can simply unbolt and replace a broken part with a new one. Medical science has found brain cells in our hearts and has tied our emotional health to our gut (microbiome) health, among other things. We are a complete system and each part of that system must be addressed—that's what holistic means: the physical and psychological.

We can often be very judgmental about ourselves and attribute our pain to our worthiness or unworthiness to heal, particularly if we already struggle with poor self-esteem. That, in turn, impacts our physical health.[2]

These aspects of ourselves—physical, mental, emotional, and spiritual—are intertwined. What happens on one level, simultaneously happens on another. What happens to our bodies, impacts our minds. What happens in our minds, how we think about things and events, directly influences the body's functioning.

What happens spiritually guides the workings of the physical. Human beings are all of these in one. For example, Michelle's healing journey has included professional coaching, journaling, meditation, prayer, and spiritual coaching.

Others on a healing journey seek their own faith and belief. The common thread among them all is the fact that healing is a process that involves looking inward.

Even though our mind, body, and spirit are interdependent, there are still activities that we can do that intentionally uplift certain aspects.

Mental and Emotional Healing

Moving from being wounded through suffering to healing is not only possible but is actually a medical preference, say researchers.[3] The word *healing* comes from the Old English *haelan* meaning *whole*. The healing journey isn't just about physical healing, these researchers claimed, but alludes to a process that brings wholeness in physical, emotional, intellectual, social, and spiritual aspects of self.

The process, referred to as "the healing journey," is facilitated by developing safe, trusting relationships. By creating positive reframing that moves through the weight of responsibility to the ability of the person to respond, amazing results happened, leading researchers to conclude that healing is not a singular event confined to a specific moment in time. Instead, it often manifests in unpredictable bursts and pauses, spanning a significant duration. This non-linear progression varies uniquely for each person on their healing journey.

Healing is a uniquely personal journey, and like any journey, is an adventure of sorts, moving at its own pace in its own time in its own way. Healing journeys can take many forms, from "individual reflection and process to dyadic therapeutic relationships to formal and informal group support, spirituality, religion, hope, self-acceptance and helping others."[4]

Is healing from a rape similar to healing from cancer, or diabetes, or inflammatory bowel disease? The disease or injuries may vary, and the degree and quality of suffering experienced by each person is more personal. The timing of their initial or ongoing wounding in the developmental life cycle and prior and current relationships also matters. Still, the bridges from suffering to healing remain the same.

In the healing journey, bridges from suffering are developed by helping people connect to healing resources/skills and helpers outside themselves. Just as in any journey, these bridges often evolve in fits and starts. They involve persistence and developing a sense of safety and trust, and the speed with which those bridges are built depends on the person, the severity, and the type of suffering to be overcome.

Between suffering and developing resources and connections, a bridge emerges. Hope, self-acceptance, and helping others occur, and healing flourishes in the pursuit of meaningful goals and purpose.[5]

Michelle's bridge, and her mental and emotional healing, started when she was forced by her cancer journey to take the time to be still and reflect. In recovery from surgery, she had six weeks of stillness. As she began to notice the emotions that arose from being instead of doing, she began intentional journaling:

> Journaling—I used to be cynical about that as well. Now, when something pops up for me, I'm trying to be disciplined in the practice of journaling and telling myself, "Okay, this popped up. Why is it popping up? What triggered it? What caused it?"
>
> A lot of the healing is trying to understand why I'm triggered and what my triggers are. Why is shadow talk happening right now? I was very closed. I didn't even want to think about it, let alone talk or write about it. That's been the beginning of the healing for me.
>
> Then I talk about it with my spirit guide. I've met with her a couple of times, and she's pulled cards and done readings for me. Yeah, it's being more open to talk about those things. It comes in bits and pieces. I knew I had an issue with trust, but I had no

idea where it came from. Then, about six months after jour-naling and trying to track my triggers, it was literally two months ago that I realized that I was raised in a family that didn't trust.

I was raised in an environment where trust was not a core value. In fact, my parents don't trust each other. My parents didn't trust us as children. They don't trust anyone else. My dad doesn't trust his family, which is why he's estranged from them.

We grew up in an environment where nobody trusted each other and my parents, especially, always felt like people were out to get them. There was constantly an attitude that people were out to get them, so there was never accountability or any of that.

Insight and healing come in waves, in bits and pieces. I'll journal about it and then I'll talk about it with my spiritual guide because I'm starting to realize the full picture of why a lot of these things exist in me. I used to just think that it was because of the former bosses I had. Now I realize I was raised not to trust. I was raised to think individually and not collectively.

Healing that trust wound is about the act of practicing trust, practicing patience. It's about responding before reacting and then trying to have the grace to be patient with myself.

As an inherent part of the process, healing requires going inten-tionally into your pain, feeling it, and moving deep into your shadow. In psychological terms, the shadow is the part of ourselves that is often hidden and unconscious. It is the uncon-scious part of the psyche that contains repressed, undesirable, or undeveloped aspects of the self. It includes aspects of ourselves that we may fear, be ashamed of, have forgotten, or are buried.[6]

Given that the shadow is still part of us, running away or neglecting the shadow creates barriers to complete self-acceptance and self-love. Thus, this is an essential part of healing, as Michelle has found:

I have a spiritual guide who helps me now. One of the things she told me to look out for is shadow talk. I had never heard the term before.

But it kept coming up until I began to notice and address it. When I'm not working, and my team is taking care of stuff—we had agreed that they wouldn't contact me and would handle things.

I had to wait to get updated when I returned to work six weeks later, after my recovery. That drove me crazy. I was chomping at the bit, wondering what was happening at work. What was going on? Was everything okay? Then the shadow talk started creeping in.

Are they doing things they're not supposed to be doing? Are they making decisions that they shouldn't be making? What if I come back and everything's a mess? What if this and what if that? At the time, I didn't know what it was. I was taking notes of the things that were bugging me."

Often, we are unaware of our underlying feelings until we tap into different parts of our bodies and the emotions they hold. Shadow work is necessary to fully feel, express, and release these emotions. It helps prevent these feelings and negative thoughts from hindering relationships and personal growth.

One way to engage in shadow work is by keeping a "shadow journal," as suggested in Robert A. Johnson's book, *Owning Your Own Shadow: Understanding the Dark Side of the Psyche.* Journaling involves noting negative thoughts, emotions, or behaviors throughout the day. Exploring this way, we can discover a connection to our whole self, unearthed subconscious thoughts and fears, and tapped into the source. Yoga also helps release pent-up emotions stored in different parts of the body, fostering synchronicity between mind and body. Each step, activity, and tool can bring greater clarity and connection with our higher self and others. Michelle explains:

> I've had several guides in my life. They've included a spiritual guide and an executive coach. Each has taught me unique lessons that shaped my thinking and path differently. Each one became a champion for me, supporting and educating me. They helped me reach awareness and push past my anger and reluctance to address my shadows.
>
> My executive coach, for instance, checked in with me when I returned to work. She was there to see how I was doing and talk through how I felt about being gone and now being back.
>
> I shared what I'd journaled about, and my coach said, "Okay, we need to talk about how much you distrust people. Where does your issue of trust come from? Why is your first gut reaction to distrust?"
>
> She nailed it. I did have trust issues, and I still do. You don't change or heal the moment you recognize a wound. It's a process. My team valiantly held down the fort during my hospitalizations.
>
> When I return for follow-ups, my team members will say, "Okay. We've got it." They have it down. Intellectually I know that, but for the six weeks I was out, my brain was swimming.
>
> Having that conversation gave me more insight, and from that I've reached out to include my spiritual guide to further help me work on my trust issues. It's a step-by-step process.

Spiritual Healing

Some may call it God, the divine, deities, Allah, the Creator. Others may call it source, love, life, spirit. Whatever you call it, spirituality of some kind is often an essential part of the healing process.

While there is much overlap and interdependence between mental and spiritual healing, the spiritual aspect of healing warrants its own discussion. The spiritual aspect of healing includes intentionally connecting with the unseen source, a higher power, or that which is all around us. Michelle's spiritual journey was an unexpected and magical one. She shares:

> While my parents were devout Catholics, I didn't have a strong spiritual belief system. However, I was intrigued by religion from a political perspective, and in college, I wrote a thesis on the gentrification of Santeria.
>
> I was on the phone, talking to my parents about my thesis, when my mother suddenly became very quiet. She said, "You need to talk to your father." My father came on the line and shared this story:
>
> "When you were three months old, you were diagnosed with pneumonia. Apparently, it was so severe that the doctors told us that there was nothing they could do for us. They advised us to pray. We are devout Catholics. We were raised to believe that the only true religion was Catholicism, but we called in a santera, a priestess, to perform a healing ritual on you."

Santeria imparts the belief that each person possesses a destiny, which can be clarified and fulfilled with the assistance and energy of the orishas, spiritual entities. This profound connection orchestrates a symphony of purpose, harmonizing mortal existence with divine guidance.

Santeria is based on the worship of these orishas and the veneration (respect and worship) of Catholic saints. Santeria is a religion with roots in West Africa and the Caribbean when enslaved Africans were brought to America. They were forbidden to practice their Yoruba beliefs. Colonialists forced them to observe Roman Catholic and Christian traditions that the colonialists were practicing.

Forming Santeria was the enslaved people's way of rebelling and incorporating their criminalized belief system (Yoruba) with the religion they were forced to embrace (Catholicism).[7] Michelle shares:

> My father went on to say, "Your life was offered to Shango. You were offered as part of the healing. If you ever decide to practice Santeria, you have to work through Shango." Shango is a deity or orisha in the Yoruba religion. He's associated with thunder, lightning, fire, dance, and justice.
>
> I'm 21, and I'm like, "Excuse me?!" It was like a movie. What? I've been offered? What are you talking about? I was never raised with Santeria in my life, but I knew about it, obviously. I had researched it in college. I knew something about the religion, but I wasn't steeped in it.
>
> Patrice (a pseudonym) is my human spiritual guide. When I first met Patrice two and a half years ago, I was sharing a story just before the pandemic hit. She practices the Trinidadian form of Santeria, and she was wearing beads. I said, "Do you pray to an orisha?" She said yes and that she was a priestess. I shared with her the story that my parents had told me about being offered to Shango.
>
> I'm telling Patrice this story, and her face turns white. I asked her, "Why are you reacting this way?" She said, "My orisha is Shango. The first time I met you, I thought your head energy read as Shango. Would you mind if I go home tonight and I pray about it?" I was like, "I don't care. Whatever." I still hadn't really gotten into it all, even with everything that was happening.

Patrice goes home, prays and prays about it, and comes back the next day with a set of beads, "You need to wear these beads. He's been waiting for you."

Again, I didn't take it seriously. I didn't wear the beads. I would pray here and there. I just wasn't really into it.

Then my cancer diagnosis came around. This was December 2019/January 2020 when these conversations were happening with Patrice. My diagnosis was in April 2021.

My diagnosis came around, and I was very open on Facebook about it. Then Patrice texted me, saying, "It's time to talk." She said, "He has put you through another initiation because you weren't taking him seriously."

I was still dealing with all the physical stuff around the cancer. It wasn't until my mastectomy and when I was spending a lot of time alone that I started to write. I also started to do these things with my executive coach. Then I said, "Oh, shit. I need to do some spirit work."

Even then, it wasn't until December 2021 that I reached back out to Patrice and said, "Okay, I'm ready now." That's when I started the whole spiritual process. That's when I started taking my service to Shango much more seriously. I start every morning with a prayer to him. I really became much more serious about it.

I was raised in a prayerful household, but I resisted it and resisted the notion of faith. My husband was raised born again Christian and has a lot of trauma from the church, so now he's an atheist.

Through the exploration of my own service to Shango, my son started paying attention to how serious I was becoming with it. We didn't raise him in a spiritual household. He would watch me pray at my altar. When he started his senior year of high school, he said, "I want to find out who my orisha is." We have been on this journey together.

It's been wild. I can't even explain it. I was always very cynical about the Catholic religion and praying to God, but praying to Shango, offering to him, asking for advice, asking for help, I don't feel any of that cynicism. I truly feel he listens. I feel his presence. It's been a wild and exciting, interesting journey.

I guess this is how people feel when they talk about faith, which is not something that I've ever had before. I would tell you I never had any sort of spiritual faith. I never believed in that. I always believed that you could pray for things, but at the end of the day, you, as a human, control the outcomes. I would never have considered having faith in something outside myself.

That's been a major part, once again, with the cancer. I must believe that treatments are working and that I'll regain good health. I have to trust that there's a path designed specifically for me and that there are valuable lessons to be learned from my journey. It's easier said than done.

Without cancer, honestly, I don't think I would have faith. As my team would tell me, I would have continued moving forward in an unhealthy, controlling manner. Cancer has compelled me to confront things I never took the time to address.

We need to lean into various practices that address healing on the physical, mental, and spiritual levels. Too often, one or two of these aspects are neglected. For example, some may complete cognitive behavioral therapy but forgo the somatic work or connection to higher power or source necessary for whole being realization, for true liberation. We can all benefit from a holistic approach, tapping into the mind, body, and spirit to heal wholly.

From Buddhism to Zoroastrianism, spirituality, religion, and faith in all sorts of things have been a part of holistic or whole-body healing practices since the beginning of time.

Over the last decade, Harvard Medical School has raised intriguing questions about religion, spirituality, and healing. "More than 3,000 studies indicate that religion (no specific religion) has a potentially beneficial effect on health," said speaker Neal Krause of the University of Michigan School of Public Health at a 2015 symposium on healing and spirituality. The symposium focused on evidence that spiritual practices like yoga, mindfulness, prayer, and practices of many kinds improved people's mental and physical health.

Regular attendance with a practicing community that is there to help members cope also helps. Community can mean any group or organization where like-minded people gather to share their beliefs, practices, and personal or professional growth.

That yoga class you go to, the meditation class, Tai Chi, weekly luncheon or coffee with friends, a therapy group, a single mom's group, the mosque, church, or temple services you attend, that foodie dinner you go to once a month to share cooking and dinner and socialization counts too. What they all provide that's essential to healing is the support of a like-minded community.[8]

Mere belief is also healing. Belief in a deity or higher power of one's preference, whether that power is encompassed in Santeria, Buddhism, Islam, Judaism, Christianity, or reincarnation, not only engenders *hope* but can connect us to a unifying force of love.

Leadership and Healing

When we heal and intentionally connect to our higher self, we can inspire, uplift others, and transcend current realities. We can also speak from a place of authenticity, intentionality, and kindness. Michelle continued:

The Heart and Healing

Healing as a leader has been challenging because control was ingrained without my awareness. This process of letting go, trusting, and questioning my actions. Is this controlling? Am I too firm with my vision? It's ongoing.

As seasoned, emerging, or potential leaders, we need to consider healing on personal and intrinsic levels as well as healing within our leadership space.

Leaders who are chained to their pain or guided by implicit negative thoughts or latent loathing (that is, unhealed leaders), often enact destructive power dynamics with their teams. Leaders with unhealed or unacknowledged trauma often lose sight of real vision, lack inspiration, and/or ignore or neglect the potential and beauty in those around them. These are the effects and impacts of unaddressed trauma. Michelle offers her insights:

As I try to let go, I tend to overcorrect. Now I'm figuring out my non-negotiables, an ongoing challenge. It's like finding myself and my voice again as a leader—a process I'm going through.

Working with my executive coach, she encouraged me to share my struggles with the executive team. I usually hesitate, thinking it burdens them. But she insists it affects them regardless, even if I don't voice it. It's been a journey of practicing vulnerability.

During my recent meeting with one of my team members, she questioned my approval of a particular thing, saying she wouldn't have approved it. Her inquiry made me reflect on my decision.

I said, "I'm struggling with what to let go of and what not to let go of and where I put my foot down. I will probably make mistakes, and I might need someone like you to tell me to rethink things."

I was very open with her, and I was very open with our VP of finance. Luckily, the world didn't end. They were gracious and said, "Thank you for letting me know. That makes sense. I'll make sure to help you with this."

Of course, they will do that because they're both lovely human beings. In my brain, I thought that if I did this, they would think I was weak. That's not what happened at all.

I've been practicing that because I'm not used to that. Also, I'm trying to determine my non-negotiables and how to get comfortable around those three or four non-negotiables. I'm working through all that with my executive coach.

When should I be inclusive? When should I ask for feedback? I always thought I was a good communicator, but then I discovered I needed to improve. I'm not good at being direct.

I'm not good at saying, "I need your input on this, but at the end of the day, I'm making the decision. I just need your input." I would never do that.

My two VPs will call you out. They will point shit out. They have no problems pointing shit out. They were the two that told me I was micromanaging. I took that as an offense. They told me separately, and I was so angry at the two of them. How dare they?

My executive coach, when I had a session with her, and I was crying and upset, she said, "What a gift. What a gift that your vice presidents will not suffer in silence. What a gift they will tell you when something bothers them."

It's been a work in progress for me to understand that they are in my life to challenge me appropriately, which is a gift. I could have just continued to create harm, not realizing it because they wouldn't tell me. Then I had to take a step back.

The Heart and Healing

It's a hell of a lot of journaling. It's looked like being vulnerable and sharing that vulnerability, especially with the organization's leadership.

I didn't realize how much my ego was tied into things—especially my leadership and relating styles. Healing for me has included learning to remove my ego and questioning myself when it comes to my ego. Instead of centering my ego, I'm trying to center my purpose. Does this feed the purpose of the foundation? Does this feed our values? I didn't always ask those questions.

It's insane how the universe works that I have both coaches in my life. In many ways, they complement each other professionally and spiritually. The questions and the challenges that they pose to me are very similar. In some ways, I'm getting it from both ends. I need to get it on both ends for it to sink in.

This practice of letting go and developing my team's leadership versus mine all of the time has been incredible. Still hard. They know it. I tell them they've got to tell me when I'm overstepping because I sometimes don't see that.

I used to have my hands in operations. I used to have my hands in administration. I used to have my hands in a lot of stuff. With my spirit guide and my executive coach, I was helped to understand that I had a real fear of letting go.

My executive coach asked, "Why are you doing all of these administrative things?" I liked it. It fed me.

She said, "Yeah, but you're the president. You shouldn't be doing these things. If we take that away, what's the fear you have?" I feared that I wouldn't know how to be a president.

I found comfort in the tactical admin that an operations person usually does. I used to be a number two and was finding myself constantly going into the number two route because I feared,

"What if I can't be this? What if I'm not strategic enough? What if I'm not visionary enough?"

The Power and Benefits of Healing

Healing can catalyze personal and professional growth, stronger relationships, fulfilling lives, and meaningful and positively impactful careers. It also means more well-rounded leadership, whole and healthy child-rearing, and thriving communities.

Healing strengthens our immune systems, clears our brain and conscience, and unifies us more with humanity. We grow in groundedness in values and a sense of who we are. We not only see ourselves in renewed ways, but also see each other as human beings.

It can help foster a sense of empowerment and self-efficacy in clients by encouraging them to take an active role in their healing process; it can improve patient outcomes by helping to address not only the symptoms of a mental health condition, but also the underlying causes and contributing factors. And it can improve overall quality of life by addressing physical, emotional, social, and spiritual needs.[9]

In an article exploring the effects of healing spaces, Zhang and team found that healing spaces can have a positive impact on patient's mental health, including reducing stress and anxiety, promoting relaxation, and improving overall well-being.[10] Michelle notes:

> One of the things you feel, if you have a tumor in your bone, is bone pain. If I picked up something too heavy, I would feel it immediately. If I bent over, I would feel it immediately. If I twisted my back, I would feel it immediately.
>
> I woke up without pain for the first time a month ago, grateful that I could move independently. I bent over to pick something

up and thought, "That doesn't hurt." I didn't think I could get ready or move again when I was hospitalized in September.

It's all those little gifts and being really grateful for my body. My body has bounced back after each treatment and each surgery. Even now, it's been four months since my back fracture happened due to the cancer. I have a scan in April, but we think the fracture has healed. I don't have any pain anymore. I can lift things that I wasn't able to lift before. I'm deeply grateful for how strong my body is.

It's taught me a lot about my own body. It's taught me a lot about what it means to be able-bodied. I've now had a couple of experiences where I wasn't. It's taught me a lot about my strength and resiliency, asking for help, being okay with receiving help, and having patience.

I also have less anxiety about the weekends. I have less anxiety about resting. I used to think rest was a waste of time. Now, I have less anxiety about resting. That became a process that was a work in progress and something for me to learn to do. I used to love being connected to work and thought that my success depended on my being connected.

I'm going to be going on vacation in mid-March and traveling. I won't be checking email. It's a journey—one step at a time.

Chapter 2: The Heart and Healing

1. What does healing mean to you, and what has it looked like in your life?
2. How can you nurture the healing you've experienced and take the next step on your journey?

Michelle Morales

Michelle Morales (she/her) is a trailblazer who has overcome significant obstacles to success in her career and personal life. Born to a working-class, military Puerto Rican family and moving around frequently as a child, Michelle became the first person in her family to attend and complete college and the first to visit Puerto Rico in nearly 50 years.

Michelle's career has been marked by a series of firsts. She is the first and only person in her family to hold a job like her current President role at the Woods Fund Chicago. This is her second job in this type of leadership position, and she has been working hard to overcome past traumas and toxic traits related to control and trust.

Michelle's personal life is equally inspiring. She is living with metastatic breast cancer, which has led her to engage in healing and spirit work. She recently started practicing Santeria and praying to her orisha, despite being raised Catholic and previously cynical about organized religion. Michelle is also married and has an 18-year-old son.

Despite her challenges, Michelle is a resilient and courageous leader committed to positively impacting her community. She inspires others facing similar obstacles and is a testament to the power of hard work, perseverance, and self-reflection.

Chapter 3
Self-Love and Finding One's Authentic Voice

Discovering your authentic voice is something that you do all the time, every day. You change. You grow. You develop. Your environment changes, grows and develops. Your values and character are also developing. More than self-worth, you want to learn about yourself and what you love, like, and need.

— Corliss Garner

As women, human beings, and WOC, we are multilayered beings. An often-stated metaphor sums up this journey of personal growth and self-discovery: "Life is like an onion. As you peel each layer one at a time, sometimes you weep." Okay, it's not all tears of pain, but tears of joy as well. There are layers about what your passions are, layers of your childhood, sexuality, spiritual connection, your coming of age, and who you are as an adult. What is happening to your subconscious under all the layers of *you,* is always changing, flowing, shifting just as the earth is layered.

The earth has a crust, which is its outermost layer. It is relatively thin compared to the other layers and is composed of solid rock—like a shell. The crust is divided into several tectonic plates that float and move on the semi-fluid layer beneath the crust, called the mantle. The mantle is the thickest layer of the Earth.

Beneath that is the outer core—a liquid layer that lies beneath the mantle. The outer core is responsible for generating the Earth's magnetic field through the movement of electrically charged materials, a process known as the dynamo effect.

Finally, there's the inner core, which is the innermost layer of the Earth, located at the very center. It is a solid sphere.

I'm not trying to take you on an earth science tour, but I wanted to use a dynamic analogy between the layers of the Earth and the layers of human personality. This can provide a metaphorical framework to understand different aspects of our inner selves. Here's a representation of these layers:

- **Crust (surface identity):** The crust of the Earth can be likened to the surface identity of an individual. Our surface identity is the characteristics, traits, and behaviors that are readily visible to others. This includes aspects such as appearance, social roles, intersectionality, and public persona. Just as the crust provides a glimpse into the Earth's composition, the surface identity offers initial insights into a person's personality but only scratches the surface. The crust is also a shell—protecting the inner self.
- **Mantle (psychological and emotional layers):** The mantle can be compared to the psychological and emotional layers of our personality. It represents the deeper aspects of an individual that shape their thoughts, beliefs, values, and emotions. Just as the mantle has a semi-fluid nature, these layers of us are not always visible to others. However, just as a shifting mantle creates earthquakes and tremors as they move, our mantle significantly influences the expression of both our

internal and external self. The psychological and emotional layers encompass our cognitive processes, subconscious influences, defense mechanisms, and personal experiences that shape a person's worldview and emotional responses.

- **Outer core (authentic self):** The outer core of the Earth is a liquid layer. It can symbolize the *authentic self* within an individual. This layer represents one's true essence, personal values, and authentic desires. It encompasses the deeper, more genuine aspects of a person's identity that may be revealed through introspection and self-reflection. The outer core holds the potential for self-awareness, self-acceptance, and the alignment of actions and choices with one's core values.

- **Inner core (spiritual essence):** Like the Earth's innermost solid core, the inner core of human personality represents the spiritual essence or the deepest sense of self. It signifies the connection to something greater than oneself, encompassing beliefs, purpose, and transcendent experiences. The inner core reflects the core of one's being, inner wisdom, and the source of inner strength, resilience, and peace.

Just as the layers of the Earth interact and influence one another, the layers of our human personality and being are interconnected and constantly in flux. The journey of self-discovery and personal growth involves exploring and understanding these layers, seeking harmony and alignment, and nurturing the connection to our authentic self and spiritual essence.

In a world where people, the government, and even our friends and colleagues don't always tell us the truth, honesty is golden. When we go to one meeting or gathering after another and hear the same lies, the carefully couched criticisms, and the vague feedback that tells us nothing about what someone is thinking, we feel a heaviness, a doubt about everything that person or organization tells us. Authenticity is often buried at the core and we must work to find it in both others and ourselves.

But once an authentic voice speaks, the haze of disbelief vanishes. The genuine expression of one's thoughts, feelings, beliefs, and experiences can move mountains.

When we describe ourselves as having an authentic voice, we're referring to our ability to communicate and engage with others in a manner that is true to ourselves, our values, and our character, without pretense or imitation.

When someone speaks of others as "being authentic," they are describing a person they perceive as being honest, sincere, and transparent about who they are and what they stand for. We trust them. We want to work with them. We want to be part of their inner circle and be fed mentally and spiritually by them because we know we hear, and see truth.

That doesn't mean the truth is always pretty or positive. It's just real. Authenticity doesn't try to influence us one way or the other. It's simply calling things what they are without trying to dress them up or diminish their darkness or wrongness. It's the truth, and we can deal with the truth, or can we?

Being Authentic Isn't Easy

Being an authentic person isn't easy. One of the primary reasons it's so difficult is we fear judgment from others. How will they perceive us? Will they criticize, reject, or disapprove of us if we don't march to their drumbeat or fall in line with popular beliefs? If we fear those things, that alone can lead us to hide or alter aspects of ourselves, suppressing our authentic voice.

As members of a group or organization that publicly stands for certain beliefs, we find our community, culture, or society has its expectations for us. There is a norm on people that shapes what is considered acceptable or desirable.

These expectations have always been around—expectations for how a WOC "should" act, or what a WOC is or isn't capable of, and how a WOC who leads should lead and what she should believe.

Those expectations can create pressure to conform. Even if they're unspoken, we know we're expected to present ourselves in ways that align with social or organizational or community standards, even if they don't truly reflect who we are. If we disagree, or refuse to buy into or parrot these expectations, we can be met with resistance, criticism, and being ostracized, making it very challenging to be authentic.

"I am woman, hear me roar!" may be how we want to present our confidence, but internal factors, such as self-doubt and insecurity, can undermine our authenticity. When called upon to speak up in a meeting, or group, or at a public event, we may question our worth, abilities, or the validity of our thoughts and feelings. Even the most self-assured, accomplished women experience self-doubt. That self-doubt can lead to a fear of being exposed or judged, causing us to hide our true selves.

Never underestimate the power of society, family, media, and culture. Throughout our lives, we are influenced by those around us. These influences shape our beliefs, values, and behaviors. There's a reason celebrities and singers, politicians and figureheads are called "influencers." They can easily lead us to conform to certain molds or roles. Expressing our authentic selves when we're the only one standing for something requires conscious effort and self-awareness.

Finally, of all the things authenticity involves, is vulnerability. We must be able to open up and share our true thoughts, feelings, and experiences, as the women who are part of the BECOME community have done in this book. Vulnerability can feel uncomfortable. Worse, it may increase the risk of rejection or emotional harm we experience. As a result, we may choose to protect ourselves by presenting an inauthentic version of ourselves.

Embracing authenticity requires self-acceptance, self-confidence, and a willingness to face potential or obvious discomfort. It involves challenging societal and community expectations and cultivating self-awareness.

Authenticity requires surrounding ourselves with supportive and accepting people who value authenticity over conformity. While finding or creating this type of group can be difficult, it's worth the search and effort. Being authentic allows for genuine connections, self-fulfillment, and a more meaningful and purposeful life. As Corliss Garner, an accomplished and empathetic organizational and social leader, learned, authenticity is a valuable ability to have, but it does come with a price. Is it a price you're willing to pay? Corliss relates:

> Settling in on what your values are, being able to shift and adapt ways that make sense for you. That's what discovering my authentic voice means. I have a niece who has been a firecracker of a kid her entire life. She has always talked about how she couldn't wait to leave the west side of Chicago, where we're from, even though her mom still lives on the west side.
>
> I want my niece to discover what hers means. Her voice may or may not be mine, but it will come from a history of women who fought to find and share their authentic voice.
>
> My mother was born in a small town in Mississippi in 1946, at the height of Jim Crow. Her parents were sharecroppers. In fact, my mother herself worked with my grandparents in cotton fields.

Self-Love and Finding One's Authentic Voice

The struggle to provide for her family meant her education suffered, limiting her to a fourth-grade education. But despite the dearth of formal schooling, she was incredibly intelligent. Now, I can't help but wonder how far she could have gone if it weren't for the rampant "isms" of her time—racism, sexism, classism—that held her back.

In the late '60s/early '70s, she, like many African Americans from the South, came to Chicago in hopes of pursuing a better life. Despite having no formal education, she found work in various domestic and healthcare roles, including as a nursing assistant.

But life in Chicago wasn't easy. She struggled to raise four children alone on her modest income. Nonetheless, she always emphasized the value of education to all of us.

Though my mother's journey was challenging, she never gave up hope for a brighter future. Her sacrifices and unwavering dedication to her family are a testament to the resilience and strength of the human spirit.

I listened to her. I was a student that wanted to do my best and gave my all. I was able to be the first in my family to graduate from college and move on to this amazing career.

My mother did end up getting her GED when she was around 40. Then she went on to get her CNA certificate and began working in nursing homes. She never made more than $15,000 a year, which is mind blowing.

When I talk about who I am, my family and my cultural lineage, I talk about it through the lens of her story.

Education has been a big passion of mine just because of my mom's story. I recognize how education can change the course of someone's life. I recognize that not only education does that, but it certainly positions someone to be more successful than their parents, grandparents, or great grandparents.

I think about education in all forms: formal education, financial literacy but also educating through mentorship, sponsorship and being an example for the next generation of Black female leaders to demonstrate to them that it is possible.

Helping my niece understand where her possibilities are and what's available to her is important to me. She's not a child that needed help speaking up, but in homing in and focusing on what she should be spending her time and attention on.

She listens and incorporates my advice, but staying on the right path requires focus and dedication. We're working on executing her plans by understanding her values and strengths and leveraging them to continue her path in life.

Whatever your dreams are, whatever it is that you have an interest or passion in, it is completely possible.

Corliss found her authentic voice through struggle, experience, and reflection, but also through the observation of and stories passed down through her mother and family. Corliss demonstrates how one's voice is also shaped by past generations, that time and family are part of who we are. That exploration of our inner selves as well as our lineage helps to tap into the unseen and undiscovered parts of self, to resurrect or ignite our potential.

When we allow ourselves to fully accept ourselves —both the light and the shadow sides of ourselves—we can come to a place of resonating with what is us instead of trying to be or be liked by someone else. When we accept ourselves and step into fearlessness, our bodies vibrate on a different frequency—the frequency of us. On this frequency, you express in words and tones that are uniquely and beautifully you—your authentic voice.

For example, when I sit in fearlessness, grounded in my center, comfortable in my space, and connected to my higher self, I speak in a deeper, fuller voice. I speak with words and phrases that are inspired by the present moment instead of regurgitations of the past. The women in our evaluations discussed their experiences of tapping into their authenticity through a journey of love, self-love, and acceptance, often facilitated by purpose, family, and healing.

Self-Love

Love itself is both a consciousness and a frequency. It's the interplay of thoughts, feelings, actions, and vibration. We believe that love exists within each and every person and all around us. It is the active and metaphysical care and perpetuation/support of life and light. It is also composed of feminine and masculine energy—light and shadow.

It is holding and soothing a crying child while trying to study, or do another task. It is listening to a friend's anguish when you'd rather be doing something else, but are committed to your friendship.

What does it look like when this thing called love is directed inward or emits from the self? Many discussions around self-love and self-care revolve around pampering ourselves, like taking baths, comfort food, breaks, or massages. While it's great to treat ourselves, true self-care comes from being authentic and truthful with ourselves.

Instead of constantly seeking outside validation or distractions, let's focus on nurturing and listening to our inner selves. By doing so, we enable the true essence of self-love to emerge and provide the healing we truly seek. This honesty helps us be more authentic, which means being truthful with ourselves about where we are, where we're going, and how we're going to get there.

Self-love means speaking to ourselves from a place of integrity and not trying to deceive or manipulate our ego or sense of self with false information that makes us feel better but doesn't help us evolve.

Self-love is bolstered by self-awareness. And self-awareness is seeing and feeling when we are authentic and when we are not. It helps us gain a deep understanding of our values, emotions, strengths, and weaknesses. It involves recognizing and embracing our unique qualities, perspectives, and experiences even if we believe no one else does.

Self-love entails establishing, communicating, and enforcing healthy boundaries with those around us. It may come with judgment and criticism, but it recognizes that those who oppose our boundaries are the ones who gain the most from our lack thereof. Self-love can also be the decision to distance ourselves from those who fail to value or respect our worth.

Self-love is a key to personal liberation. By cultivating unconditional positive regard towards ourselves, we discover our own world while also learning to appreciate and love others more completely.

Through the journey of self-love, we realize that you and I are one. By truly loving and accepting ourselves, we naturally extend love and acceptance towards others. This creates a powerful foundation for leading teams and movements rooted in loving kindness.

Self-love encompasses more than just self-acceptance: it is also about self-care, self-consideration, and self-exploration. As we embark on this journey, we can visualize it as a well: at the top, we enter the darkness of the tunnel. But at the bottom, we find the water of love, which sustains, surrounds, and nourishes us.

When we get through the darkness, to the water, we're immersed. Thus, at the end of this journey is just love. We love ourselves and everyone and everything else. We're just in love. In this space, we are liberated—from distortion, from hate, from insecurity, from oppression, from dogma, from the effects of harm.

Self-love doesn't always feel warm and fuzzy or even desirable. Self-love means accepting ourselves as a whole, embracing both our positive and negative aspects. We acknowledge and embrace our flaws, imperfections, and past mistakes without judgment or self-criticism. We are who we are, and that's okay because it's a starting place for healing, for power, for self-care.

Psychologist Carl Rogers wrote primarily about self-love, self-care, self-actualization, and the search for an authentic personality. He advocated for people to live authentically by openly expressing their true thoughts, feelings, and desires. One of his best-known quotes is, "The curious paradox is that when I accept myself just as I am, then I can change."

Overall, Rogers emphasized the importance of self-acceptance, self-expression, and trusting one's own experiences as foundational aspects of self-love. His perspective of self-love involves several key elements, the first of which he is most known for: unconditional positive regard.

Rogers believed that individuals should cultivate a deep and unconditional acceptance of themselves, including their strengths, weaknesses, and emotions. Regarding self-love, he urged people to embrace themselves with compassion and without judgment. This first involves acknowledging your inherent worth and valuing oneself regardless of external achievements or conditions.

This genuine self-expression Rogers encouraged involves being honest with yourself, being true to your values and needs, and not conforming to external expectations from others not committed to your healing and growth. Corliss also came to this insight through her life journey:

Coming into a better understanding of who you are in this moment—that means all of what you are, your successes, your shortcomings, your failures, your values, the things that you hold dear. But still recognizing that even with all of that, you bring something unique to the world, your community, and whatever space and place you hold and occupy.

For me, understanding all of that, recognizing that to be loved does not mean to be perfect and to accept those things about yourself and navigate the world in a way that you can still bring your own uniqueness to it. That's how I think through self-love.

I think you're always discovering. I believe that your authentic voice is something that you continue to evolve into. I never discount the power of growing older and having life experiences that teach you so much.

I turn 50 this year. I think when folks hit some sort of milestone birthday, it causes you to pause and reflect. For me, being on the earth for half a century, I think about where I was 30 years ago and what my maturation level was. Where was it 20 years ago? Ten years ago? Everything that I have learned along that journey continues to prepare me to walk into this era of self-love, understanding all of the strengths and imperfections and still knowing that I still have a lot to contribute.

By living authentically and reflecting, we can foster a sense of self-love and personal fulfillment. Neither Rogers nor Corliss said it would be easy, but both agree it would be life-changing.

Healing and self-care facilitate finding our authentic voice and make it easier to step into that more often. We heal by engaging in activities that promote our well-being, such as setting healthy boundaries, exercising, healthy eating, restful sleep, engaging in hobbies, and seeking therapy or counseling. We also learn what self-love truly is, and that includes times when we don't feel so great about ourselves but know we're doing what's good for ourselves.

Self-care is the aspect of self-love that includes actively taking care of our physical, emotional, and mental health. The next time you go to the gym, run or work out and feel hot, tired, sweaty, and maybe even frustrated, that's self-care.

When you set and enforce a boundary with a child, or co-worker, or friend and they get angry and stomp off, or leave, or yell at you, that's self-care—setting and enforcing your personal boundaries.

These are the times when self-love involves being as kind and compassionate towards ourselves as we are to those we love. The greater the challenge or setback, the more we need to treat ourself with the same understanding, patience, and empathy that we would extend to a loved one.

Practicing self-love is an ongoing process that requires patience, self-reflection, and self-compassion. It involves cultivating a positive and nurturing relationship with yourself, recognizing your worth, and prioritizing self-care and well-being. By fostering self-love, we can enhance our overall happiness, resilience, and ability to form healthy and fulfilling relationships with others. Corliss offers the following insights about the power of reflective practice and its connection to relationships:

> One of the things I try to do is a self-check. Reflection on experiences, relationships, especially difficult relationships. I always ask myself what my role was and what I could have done differently. I'm open to hearing that feedback. Sometimes that doesn't feel good. I well up the courage and take the time to sit back and listen and then reflect on what I hear. That creates more self-awareness.
>
> It's not just about journaling or any particular activity. It's about that self-reflection. Sometimes, I think back on relationships and

situations, and I pause and say, "Could I have handled that differently? Could I have taken a different tone?" I check in with my boyfriend and say, "Could I have done something differently?"

If you are reflective, you can see common things in terms of relationships. It's a tool to learn about who you really are.

In learning and accepting who we really are, we can liberate ourselves from societal stressors and physical limitations. We can create a world for ourselves that is surrounded by love and love emanating from us in every direction. Through this inner journey, we also create pathways for others' liberation. As Marianne Williamson so eloquently stated in her book *A Return to Love,* "As we are liberated from our own fear, our presence automatically liberates others." And so, as we tap into the love within, others experience that love around us.

Chapter 3: Self-Love and Finding One's Authentic Voice

1. What are three things you genuinely love about yourself?
2. What part of yourself needs more care and tenderness?
3. What truth from your life do you wish to share with the world?

Corliss Garner

Corliss Garner (she/her) is a seasoned professional serving as the chief diversity, equity, and inclusion officer at Old National Bank. Throughout her impressive career, she has been a trailblazer in the area of corporate social responsibility and diversity, equity, and inclusion. This industry leader celebrates noteworthy experience from her prior roles, the most recent being the head of corporate social responsibility and diversity, equity, and inclusion at First Midwest, which merged with Old National Bank in 2022.

With over two decades of experience at BMO Harris Bank, Corliss has excelled in numerous leadership positions. Her academic background is equally impressive, including a bachelor's degree in finance from DePaul University. Renowned for her sharp intellect, Corliss holds certifications as a financial planner and trust and financial advisor. She not only contributes actively to the community through philanthropy, but also serves as a life director and previously chaired the advisory board for the Chicago Community Trust African American Legacy Fund. Additionally, she has served on the boards of Chicago State University, the Executive Service Corps of Chicago, and the DePaul University Coleman Entrepreneurship Center. Corliss's exceptional experience and unwavering commitment to public service are unparalleled, and her professional achievements are truly commendable.

Chapter 4
Healing Practices for Organizations

On June 7, 2014, I phased into a transformational journey called motherhood. I gave birth to a 6.4-oz baby girl named Naevia (Nay-vee-uh) Miller. This milestone shifted my inner compass, mindset, and life priorities because ever since I have been learning the evolutionary side of being a mommy, co-parenting and raising our daughter in another city outside of our hometown.

— Shemeka Woodson

Shemeka was also a new team member at BECOME, a graduate student and—like all of us at that time—working remotely because of COVID-19. If that wasn't enough to deal with, Naevia began having headaches. As she shares:

It all started when Naevia came home from summer camp complaining of a headache. At first, it was eased with a generic over-the-counter children's Tylenol and her favorite treat, a popsicle. But it started to get worse.

Initially, we responded by ruling out the general causes of headaches. Since her illness began at a time when her dad and I were laid off because of COVID-19, our family didn't have health insurance, so we used alternative home remedies first. After some time, Naevia was finally approved for Children's Medicaid, which allowed for a doctor's visit and referral to a neurologist. At that time, we were told she was dealing with 'migraines with aura' because she reported a tingly sensation over her body whenever a headache began.

After asking for an MRI, I was told that these scans don't always reveal the origin of a migraine and should be the last resort in her plan after trying out the medicine. We followed directions for a special diet to prevent migraines and began a migraine medication that honestly didn't seem to work. I started researching known herbal remedies like Nettle Leaf and began to incorporate herbal baths and teas into her daily routine.

Naevia was always a petite child but seemed to be losing weight and her headaches progressed with intensity and frequency. She was uncontrollably crying with head pain, almost daily. It got to the point that Naevia was waking up with headaches, so it was clear something was wrong, and these recommendations were not working. After weeks of frustration, I took her to the Emergency Room and urged them to do an MRI and lab work because I truly didn't know what else to do. What we thought might be a weekend venture to the ER turned into a long, daunting discovery and journey.

Although her lab work appeared normal, besides slight iron deficiencies, her unexplained weight loss and MRI scan of the brain raised some serious red flags. We were transferred from the ER to an inpatient room while we waited for further news from the neurologist. I remember that follow up meeting like a recurring nightmare. The cold room, my clammy hands, my shaking body, and tight throat as the doctor reported that the abnormal scans revealed an unidentified layering of cells resting on different parts of Naevia's brain. I had fearful burst of tears and screams as her dad and I held each other in a fit of shock and disbelief. That doctor's words echoed in a loop in my head, but I still needed to find the strength to walk back into my baby's hospital room with a calm face to comfort her. I wiped away my tears and somehow managed to compose myself enough to walk in with a smile on my face, ready to stay by her side.

As a freelance contractor at the time, I halted all my projects and prepared to make the necessary sacrifices to see my baby through to the other side. Prior to this ER visit, I recently agreed to a contract with a new client, BECOME, as the Executive Assistant for the organization. I remember wondering if I was going to have any source of income to maintain our rent and bills after all this.

In the context of a company, workplace, or even a neighborhood block, a healing organization prioritizes the well-being and holistic development of its employees, peers, or neighbors. It goes beyond the traditional focus on productivity and profitability and aims to create an environment that supports its people's physical, emotional, and psychological health.

A healing organization recognizes that the well-being of members is crucial for their overall engagement, satisfaction, and effectiveness in the work or living space. BECOME is such an organization. We promote a positive and supportive work culture that encourages open communication, trust, and psychological safety —as well as collaboration among team members. When Shemeka joined BECOME, she was facing multiple issues, several of them unexpected and immensely challenging. We were all dealing with COVID-19 restrictions and working remotely. That was both a blessing and a challenge for parents with young children. Shemeka describes her journey:

My vibrant baby girl was a sassy mini version of myself, teaching me new perspectives on life and allowing me to view beauty through the eyes of a child. I've been learning all the tricks and trades of motherhood, co-parenting, co-existing, and this rapid growth in personal development and leadership. I've also been exploring myself, the type of mom that I want to become, and how that's inter-connected with my partner. Accepting the ebb and flow of this process has been a transcendent experience. It has its challenges, of course, but overall, it's been a wonderful season of revelations.

Despite all that we'd gone through prior to 2021, there was no way to foresee what was to come.

While in the hospital, Naevia admitted to pretending to eat her food the past few months at home but really had been secretly giving it to our dog or throwing it away because she simply did not feel hungry. This was later explained as a side effect from the placement of abnormal cells on her brain that were indeed affecting her appetite regulation.

Her diagnostic testing phase seemed prolonged because, aside from her malnutrition and weight loss, most other test results were showing up nearly average or normal even though the MRI scans indicated there was clearly something wrong. Our last resort was to undergo the invasive surgery of two brain biopsies to test the abnormal cells. This led us to the pathology results.

Ultimately, she was diagnosed with a rare brain tumor—clinically known as a diffuse leptomeningeal glioneuronal tumor. Ironically, I received the pathologist report of that second biopsy while in the hospital on my birthday in 2021. They confirmed that we were dealing with abnormal glial cells found in sections of the cervical spinal cord, brain stem, and other parts of her brain. Throughout her unexpected hospitalization, I remained a strong mama warrior and heavy advocate on behalf of Naevia, coordinating with multiple teams of doctors working to figure out what was happening to my child.

Shemeka didn't have to face what came next alone. Since founding BECOME, my aim has been to foster an environment where team members can thrive, evolve, and give their best to the world. I wanted a place reflective of the harmonious society we aspire toward, one that's loving, empathetic, ennobling, and inspiring—a healing sanctuary where people of color can step into life-changing leadership. Experiencing it for oneself is incomparable to mere vision, goal, or reverie. By intentionally practicing leadership, healing, loving, and more, we can make it real.

My aim was for the team to witness, appreciate, and cultivate spaces that embodied the power of healing, guidance, and compassion. Here, the emphasis is on actively promoting healing. By taking a proactive approach, you can establish spaces, communities, organizations, neighborhoods, or even streets that foster a sense of healing. When we ask for those things, we very often get them.

To bring this vision to life at BECOME, it was paramount to create processes that helped healing, spaces that supported it, and opportunities that nurtured it. Our relationships needed to encourage such an environment that allowed healing with time and space for love. A "healing organization," wasn't just an idea or a theory. With Shemeka, it became real. She and her daughter needed us, and we needed them.

This has been a practice, a journey in learning, challenge, and growth. At our organization, we've implemented personal peace days. The last Friday of every month, the team is allotted a paid day to focus on self-care. It's a space in which we're free to design our day as we please, with activities ranging from massage sessions to nap-taking. Such wellness practices are essential for the healing of organizational culture.

Healing Practices for Organizations

To develop a loving and kind environment, start with an eternal mindset, free from limited deadlines and time constraints, one that exudes patience and is focused on processes that unravel, reveal, discover, and uplift both ourselves and each other.

To create a space for healing, build on the foundation of consciousness by implementing processes and policies that facilitate growth. This can range from a basic employee wellness program to a more elaborate routine of collective reflection and exploration.

Such a space should encourage people to coach each other toward unlocking their inner greatness. It should allow each person to step into their potential and manifest their vision. This journey entails cultivating certain skills and characteristics that enable growth in a healing space. Ultimately, the characteristics of a healing space are multifaceted: inclusive, supportive, uplifting, and transformative.

Creating time and space for growth and personal development or healing journeys, such as Shemeka's journey with her daughter and family, is vital. We have an internal group dedicated to facilitating and supporting both the professional and personal development of our team and others. We also have collective development paths and personal vocational journeys that are supported by the organization: time, talent, and treasure.

Holding time and space for person-to-person connection is also essential—as we'll learn in the next section, positive relationships also heal. Because positive relationships can be a conduit for healing, we feed into group and one-on-one relationship building through encouraging everything from lunches to in-depth mediation through conflict.

It's important to support the whole person to thrive, not just one aspect of that person (like them as a worker or activist or artist). We don't see people we work with as workers or employees. We're people. We're human beings. "Work" is just one aspect of our lives, one manifestation of expression or striving for something — be it survival or flourishing or purpose. Healing often takes more time than we'd like, encompasses more areas than we realized, and becomes an unexpected journey down paths we didn't see ahead of us, as Shemeka describes:

> Self-Healing? I didn't feel like I had time to think about it. I told myself, "I've got to keep moving and just do everything I can to make sure my daughter is okay." I was in denial that I needed to take a breath. But that denial didn't take away the impact that this trauma had on my body and my mental state. I had this profound feeling that a pot was boiling over. Whether it was my productivity, my inner voice, or my soft addictions, I was neglecting the practices that once connected me to source and peace.

> Three years prior, I was heavy into meditation, prayer, oracle card readings, and altar work. I grew into honoring the elements around me. I was committed to staying grounded and connected to that ether space and energy outside of this physical avatar. It was as if I subconsciously started neglecting these core spiritual practices and thought, "I just don't know if I have time for that now." For some reason, it reminded me too much of the insurmountable pain.

> My faith in self was pushed to the limit; my faith in God was tested in so many ways.

> Shortly after her confirmed diagnosis, we were moved to the floor for all cancer patients. "If you say these are your beliefs, now is your time to live and leap boundless in it," I told myself. "If this is who you say you are, your faith in God and your connection to the spirit realm, now is the season to rest upon that soul work." I created a healing atmosphere by writing scriptures, affirmations, and high vibrational words on the room wall

to cast an undeniable proclamation of life over my daughter. I created a mini altar in the hospital room for daily prayer and meditation with her spirit guides to intercede and bring forth her healing.

My acknowledgment for healing began with numbness and resistance because I was responding to this stressful situation from a surface level place. Post the hospitalization, months later, my healing process turned into a full surrender to the experience and my thoughts about it, the present moment, and my feelings around it.

My spiritual transformation elevated once I leaned into living an attitude of gratitude in all aspects of my life, especially the ones that hurt. It's through the painful moments that you remember your strength and how to endure and develop perseverance for this cyclic energy experience called life. You must learn to embrace life.

This Texas-raised educated Black girl mom and entrepreneur just so happened to align with BECOME for a divinely timed connection. I am grateful that I connected with BECOME at a point in my journey that allowed me to bear witness to the true power and liberation of supportive community networks. BECOME and our team played a role in showing me the concept of actualizing your own vision and circumstances outside of your existing reality. Continuing to hold space as the newest BECOME team member during this delicate time for my family allowed me a place of serenity and a sense of positive distraction of living in a hospital during my daughter's two-month diagnostic hospitalization.

BECOME organically aided me by providing room where I could find solace and regain some sense of control when I felt helpless in other aspects of my life. In the chaotic midst of coordinating medical procedures, tests, and uncertainty, I found comfort and release through the reflective meeting check-ins, critical reflection spaces, purposeful heart work, and abundant support from the team.

This temporary sense of escape from the hospital environment allowed me to recharge, gather my thoughts, and be in a better mental state to support my daughter. While I did everything I could to get my daughter better, including relocating back to our hometown to be closer to her medical team, family, and friends, I discovered that my own self-care was sorely lacking. BECOME's emphasis on holistic healing, wholeness, and self-care aligned very deeply with my path and was even more needed in this time.

One very simple, small, yet powerful way we acknowledge each other, and the healing we're going through, is through our check-ins. We start every meeting with a check-in, such as "how are you arriving," to hear and convey that humans are coming into space —humans that have multifaceted lives, needs, and experiences that influence their state and trajectory at any given time.

One of my favorites is PIES: how people are doing Physically, Intellectually, Emotionally, and Spiritually. I forget the original source of this but thank you to whoever developed it. We also acknowledge this in the way we typically greet each other — with a hug and/or a how are you, staying to listen to the real answer.

Integrating whole life conversations (e.g., check-ins to start meetings on how people are arriving) into the work or purpose space alone creates more grounding and connection. In addition to the check-ins, this includes space dedicated to reflection, authentic connection, and group discussion.

For example, we have a "movement building dreamspace" where we connect as a team, delve into deep issues facing the community, about life, within each other, or imagining our future.

We are all leaders—in different stages of learning, healing, and growing. We come to the space with some skills, no skills, new skills, old skills—dedicated to learning, practicing, and supporting each other in those skills as we all grow into more effective leaders.

Skills Needed to Be a Healing Leader

Healing leaders are facilitators. They are able to facilitate spaces and discussions for deeper connection, discovery, and self and collective realization.

They're listeners, hearing both the spoken word, as well as unspoken, the deeper meaning, hopes, yearnings, and desires of people. A healing leader sees where and who people are in the moment as well as their potential. They see the potential or the best in people, even when the person can't see it themselves.

They don't just see that potential; they hold and reflect or mirror the best in them. They co-create a path to self-knowledge and realization. The journey and the path to healing can be complex. Leaders often must learn on the fly, just as their team does. When Shemeka was learning to navigate her child's cancer, work, relationship, and her new job, we learned with her.

Shemeka was able to get through that time with us. Part of it was working with us and knowing she had a team to plug into. We still created space and supported her through the process. Patience is also a part of that because it was a lot that she had to go through. There was the time and intensity and emotional agony of it. We were still there throughout the whole experience. Shemeka expounds:

> Reaching a diagnosis was a process. Naevia's dad and I took her to the hospital for what we thought was going to be maybe a weekend of testing, get the medicine, and be done. A one-day appointment turned into two months in the hospital, first in

San Antonio and then an air flight to Houston, for another 45 days or so.

She began to have some serious reactions to the various medicines. Upon admittance, her intracranial pressure was double the normal amount and we needed to relieve that pressure with multiple spinal taps. She began to experience involuntary emesis as the result of a medicine which spiraled into her not being able to eat by mouth in the hospital. She was scared she would vomit, and, in many instances, she did.

Her emotional regulation was affected by the placement of the tumor cells so she was easily agitated and fragile. She was emotionally sensitive. She began reporting a burning sensation versus a prickling pain when she had headaches which indicated that she was having nerve pain. We hadn't experienced these things as patients but as her parents. This meant we experienced them for the first time through the eyes of a parent, feeling helpless in being able to shield her from these things, all the while knowing much of the process was necessary to get to the answer.

The pathology report started the path towards the journey of the "treatment plan." After a huge transition of living in a hospital for two months and being mom, caregiver, and prayer warrior, I broke down to my knees in the hospital room crying and praying for help.

It took them a while to successfully manage her pain outside of the separate issue of diagnosing her. It had been over a month of trying to manage the excruciating head pain and the suffering. I felt as though I had nowhere else to go. I was doing all I knew to do and all I was ever taught to do. We come to the hospital when you're medically ill and don't know what's going on. How do we still not know how to help her? Those were the thoughts that were going through my mind in those moments.

I recall one night Naevia's pain was so severe for her little body that she broke down and said very weakly, "Mommy, I really am just tired of the headaches, and I don't think I can do this anymore. I would rather die to make them stop." My heart still aches and breaks from that moment in time. I had to endure and see my child experience a trauma that I didn't know how to stop.

I had never been in this situation before, so I have no idea what the resolution was supposed to be. All I knew was to be present. All I knew was to love. All I knew was to seek power outside of myself for the comfort that both of us needed in that space and time.

We agreed to use an experimental targeted chemotherapy. Naevia was discharged from the hospital with a rare pediatric cancer diagnosis, an ongoing treatment plan and morphine as the only viable pain management. She had a gastrostomy button (G-button) placed in her tummy to help feed her, but her prescriptions were causing other adverse side effects that we now have to tackle. It was a whirlwind of stressful situations all occurring at one time. Navigating all of that has been one of the most challenging times of my life.

I'm not just navigating through that for myself: I'm navigating through for my daughter as her guardian, as the person that she selected to guide her through this journey and help her. The responsibility and the accountability that I felt in that fact was very heavy.

Leaders often lead because of their vision, and their hope. They think in visionary ways about reality – about people, groups, organizations, communities and/or society. A healing leader supports, voices, and facilitates vision, visioning, and visionary thinking on multiple levels. Each year, we kick off with our visioning for the year, including having each person vision for themselves as well as the organization.

A healing leader not only taps into logical reasoning but into their intuition—their heart knowledge and deeper spiritual knowing. Along the way, I've seen many of our team grow in their leadership, like Shemeka. She leads within the organization as much as she is leading her family through challenges and hardships. I've learned our personal lives are very often where our best and most challenging learning opportunities come from. As Shemeka shares:

> This entire experience has been an intense, vulnerable, and unearthing journey. I was the first witness to seeing my child endure all that she has at the tender age of seven years old. She has endured the hospitalization, six surgeries, 15 scans, adverse medicine side effects like dystonia and vomiting. She now must process living in a new city as a childhood cancer patient with an emotionally and physically taxing treatment plan. She's continuing the work to overcome her anxiety and post-traumatic stress. Now, she illuminates as this vibrant, inspiring nine-year-old girl who loves to sing, dance, and play Roblox. She's astonishingly open about her testimony and being a child with cancer.
>
> You truly never know what people are going through. I have the vision to see how monumental being a part of her journey is going to be in her life story. That excites me. It makes me warm on the inside, as a mom and as a human being, to know somebody who has endured so much pain at a tender age and to see the phases of their recovery to the other side. It has changed me for the better to see her prevail past all that she has gone through in two years and show up to be as compassionate and empathetic as she is still for others. She did not let the feelings of defeat strip away her strong spirit.
>
> The power that she owned in all of this was staggering to me. My child would come to me when I was breaking down crying on the hospital bed and wipe my tears away. She would say in a calm, wise voice, "Mommy, you don't have to cry for me. I'm

going to be okay. God's going to take care of us." "Mommy, I hear you on the phone and I know you say you're worried, but you don't have to worry about me because we're going to be okay. Don't you know that?" She was this still yet powerful voice to reaffirm my faith. She was tapping into a knowingness about Spirit and God that we all have. I believe there is an inherent wisdom that children can tap into that we as adults often forget. She, at the tender age of seven, tapped into what I, at 33, was unable to at the time. That is remarkable and ethereally humbling. My pride comes from being able to bear witness to my daughter's emerging holistic transformation.

As far as continuing my journey, I've grown to acknowledge and actively put into practice the necessary self-work in healing this trauma. That's included exploring, reflecting, and restoring the areas of self that were affected so I can be the best reservoir of love for her.

I'm seeking to know thyself. I came to the realization that I was neglecting my spiritual practices. I was ashamed to admit it, but it was as though parts of me grew resentful of God for allowing our family to go through that. I'm seeking to let go of the guilt that I have, feeling as though I was supposed to know what was going on with her even before we officially knew what was going on. I thought I should've known just because I'm the mama. I've ultimately felt responsible for the suffering and pain that my child went through for months when we didn't know that it was a tumor causing her headaches. I've spent many nights in solitude with crying spells asking for forgiveness, in my naivety.

There were all these different theories being thrown at us, and I tried my best to navigate through the fluff to an answer. However, I still couldn't help feeling as though, had I figured out a resolution earlier, my child would not have undergone such an agonizing first and second grade. Although I continue to hear repeatedly the encouragement of others in my circle saying,

"How could you have known? No one should automatically jump to that extreme when your child comes to you and says they have a headache. That's not on you to have known that."

I still needed to discover and realize, in my own heart, that it is not my weight or burden to carry because it was the will of The Most High. It was meant for Naevia to endure this unique experience in her journey and to share her story. She had to go through to break through. This testimony is greater than me or her. This testimony will stand to be a reason why someone else gets faster help. I believe that we were selected for this path because a higher power knew that we would be able to endure, to tell this story, and inspire others so that many families facing unexplained childhood cancer can know they are not alone.

We are a part of something greater than ourselves. I embrace the fact that the healing process is a continuum with a revolving door. I am evolving as a mom, as a human, as a black woman, and a leader. I've gone through despair and feeling helpless, yet I do remain hopeful. My healing journey has seen some darkness, self-doubt, disbelief, distrust, pain, anger, sadness, defeat, withdrawal, fear. It all pushes me to the revelation of who I really am. My belief in the power of prayer, my convictions, my energy healing abilities, and my faith all represent dynamic elements of Shemeka.

We live in a limitless and boundless realm for energy made to flow, in whatever direction you will it to go. I unwaveringly stand solidly by the vision of Naevia's complete healing and our family. And so, it shall come to pass. I will continue to instill wisdom and foster development for her intuitive mind. We must learn how to be in this world but not of it. It was a reawakening for me.

Even amid profound fear, darkness, pain, and self-doubt, Shemeka rose as an amazing mother and leader. Our organization learned and grew through her deepened connection to herself, her daughter, and to source. In many ways, organizations and blocks are groups of people and our lived and work experiences become part of the DNA of the organization. Through everyone's trials and triumphs, we witness, support, and uplift for the good of that person and the good of all.

Chapter 4: Healing Practices for Organizations

1. Where have you experienced healing spaces—at home, in your neighborhood, or professionally?
2. How have (or could) you fostered moments of healing for others?

Shemeka Woodson

Shemeka Woodson (she/her) is a nonprofit management professional and a collaborative community change agent who is passionate about people empowerment, human capital, and serving marginalized populations. She carries eight-plus years of administrative and managerial experience with a versatile skill set ranging from data entry, project management, program management and evaluation, grant writing, branding/marketing, and social media management.

A Houston native, she began working in the nonprofit sector as an affordable housing advocate in social services management for low-income residents and families in South Texas. She has served on the City of San Antonio's Community Action Advisory Board as a private representative in 2016. Shemeka also owns Colorful Conscience LLC, a socially conscious business branding purposeful work to IGNITE change, INSPIRE communities, and IMPACT the next generation using collaborative alliances within the public and private sectors. Her mission is to address the social determinants of health by creating bridges for people-

powered solutions that ignite social equity and change.

She holds a bachelor of arts in sociology from St. Mary's University (San Antonio), a community health worker certification from the State of Texas, and a nonprofit leadership and management graduate certificate. She also pursued her master's in public administration from the University of Texas–San Antonio.

She is a dedicated mother, leader, and inspirer and has contributed to molding a healing and values-centered culture at BECOME.

Section Two

Relationships: Developing and Deepening Strong Connections

All human beings, regardless of gender, color, or culture have the same innate need: we long to belong. And belonging means relationship. The term *relationship* often conjures one of three scenarios in people's minds: work, love, and the world around us —the people we welcome with open arms, those we collaborate with, and those we approach with caution until they've proven themselves. Relationships embody both safety and growth as they shape our interactions with the world and everyone in it.

The seeds for this book are rooted in the idea of relationship: the connection between people, on teams, from institution to institution, from institution to people, and within communities. This concept transcends people and situations and enters realms both quantum and cosmic.

Every connection between "us" and "them" is a relationship. The only difference is the kind of relationship it is. There are relationships among things, people, entities, colors, and even memories or ideas. Everything in life constitutes a relationship. It's the relationships between things and people, and people and others that create our reality. This book is a relationship—between the women telling their stories, and the people reading them.

Relationships can be casual, shallow, deep, intimate, platonic, professional, or personal—positive or negative. They can be close or distant, virtual or literal. Two entities can be in a relationship despite physical or emotional distance, like estranged ex-partners or coworkers. These relationships still hold influence, whether on past thoughts and behaviors or present avoidance.

When thinking about relationships in work, community, family, and otherwise, we need to consider the distance between others, as well as the reason and purpose for and of the relationship.

Chapter 5
The Importance of Relationships on Every Level

Someone told me a powerful story about a janitor. I've never forgotten it. It sums up the importance of relationships for me.

This janitor was a Black guy who had been around a long time. Everybody in the building knew him. This is when companies used to have people come around pick up the mail and clean your office. This was also when everything was written down on paper—before email and all of that.

He was a well-known and well-liked person in the company. Why? Because he was always helpful and friendly to everyone he interacted with daily. He said hello to people. He paid attention to what people did and where they worked. He cared about the company. He didn't just empty trash and mop floors, even if that's what most people assumed—he was, after all, "the janitor."

One day, the company sent out a notice that they had a new supervisor position to fill. After careful consideration, a highly capable Black woman was selected as the new supervisor. The janitor noticed this. Day after day she'd come in and walk to her office, nodding to him if he said hello, but never stopping to actually talk to him. It wasn't that she wasn't a friendly person. She wasn't trying to be rude. She simply said, "I don't have the time."

What she was really thinking was, "He's the janitor. I don't want them (her White coworkers) to see me interacting with the janitor because then they won't hold me in high esteem. They'll think that I'm at 'his level,' and not worthy of my office."

She was embarrassed and made assumptions, like assuming he had nothing of value to offer her because he was the man who emptied the trash and collected the garbage. She was an executive.

What she didn't realize was that because he was the one that emptied the trash and collected all the garbage, he had access to all the memos and notes in the CEO's garbage.

One night after emptying the trash, he learned the company was doing some restructuring that was going to impact this Black woman and her job. After that, he tried to get to her to share what he'd found out. He wanted to give her a heads up about what was happening, maybe give her time to prepare herself, or defend her job, and not be blindsided.

He tried to walk up to her the next morning. She nodded at him and kept on walking, fearful someone would see them talking. All he was trying to do was give her the 411 on what was going on. He never got the chance.

She missed an opportunity and lost her job.

— Georgina Heard-Labonne

So many things can get in the way of a relationship: fear, misperceptions, preconceived ideas about people, and stereotypes. So many melanated women we've talked with over the years have confessed to suffering from imposter syndrome. They think they're not good enough, accomplished enough, or smart enough to have the position or win the award, or to make the ideal amount of money.

I was in a workshop a few years ago that helped women tell their story in a way that was confident and truthful, not self-deprecating or devaluing. Essentially, they asked us to brag. They asked us to tell a small break-out group about our accomplishments, skills, talents, and recognitions. It was very awkward at first but the more we talked, the more at ease and expansive we felt.

If you think that because you're too old, too young, not degreed, not powerful, not a leader, not rich, too poor, from a "bad" background or not a good enough background, you have nothing to bring to a relationship, you're wrong.

Most people in Western culture have been conditioned to perceive the world as fragmented, disconnected, and void of any sense of relationship outside of that which obviously benefits them financially or personally.

While there are many tactics used to get in the way of real relationships, the construct of race is one of the biggest and most debilitating examples of cohesion blockers. It has been used to create not just a separation among the human race—but to create a hostile, volatile, violent competition. This separation is a fabricated contest among groups based on the shade of our skin.

The result is a distorted reality where people miss the fact that everything and everyone exists within a unified field. We want to step outside this win/lose paradigm and into this unified field of culture and community where all human beings, of all skin colors, ethnicities, and belief systems, are respected, included, and most of all—valued for themselves.

Despite the apparent lack of connection at times, there is a pervasive force that flows through everything and binds us together. We can move into a practical utopia that many of our ancestors imagined: a community where we love each other beyond color, beyond pain, beyond judgment, beyond actions, and into existence, where we see, hear, listen, and uplift each other to complete being.

To achieve a reality where relationships overcome race, we must give birth to a different leadership paradigm. A relationship-focused society requires a different mindset and a different consciousness.

Seeing the big picture as well as the connections of the pieces within it is an important characteristic of this needed mindset. We must cultivate relational thinking to avoid making false assumptions and misguided decisions based on limited or decontextualized reasoning. For instance, the East-West Comparison Study, also known as the Michigan Fish Test and the Framing Effect Study, explored cultural differences in perception and decision-making. The research investigated how American and Japanese people responded to visual stimuli, by first using a picture of a large fish in an underwater scene in a pond.

Researchers found that American participants tended to focus more on the focal object (the fish) and made choices based on the fish's features. On the other hand, Japanese participants paid greater attention to the overall scene, such as plants, the landscape, and the big picture. They tended to make choices based on contextual relationships.

This study and other research related to it highlight how culture shapes cognitive processes and thinking styles. Culture influences us in areas such as perception, attention, and decision making. It affects the role of context we adopt in shaping cognitive processes.

Cultural conditioning significantly influences our perceptions and ways of thinking. Americans attributed the fish's behavior to an inherent trait, while the Japanese saw it as a result of contextual information—that the fish acted as it did because of where it was, not what it was.

Personally, as someone with an American background, I think the Japanese interpretation is more accurate. Our actions are influenced by situational context, in addition to our knowledge, personality, and past experiences.

It's important that we interrogate our cultural context and influences, especially around relationships. These cultural forces can keep us from important relationships, as we saw in the story Georgina conveyed, or guide us into belonging and love. At the core of how we live is our relationship with people in our lives and the contexts of those relationships.

Understanding the various levels of relationships in your life is key to becoming a change maker. These levels refer to the relationships between:

- You and other people in your space
- Members within a team or group, be it an organization, community, or neighborhood
- Your own group in relation to other groups doing the same or different things

Moreover, our relationship with ourselves is the foundation for all other levels and deserves attention too. To become a true change maker, it's important to nurture our interactions at every level.

Through our evaluation work, the women, be it in community organizing, philanthropy, or nonprofit organizations, tended to relationships on each level to realize the change they wanted to see. They also tended to these levels in their own development and well-being.

The Impact of Relationships

Have you ever missed an opportunity because you lacked a relationship? Did you not hear of a job, a position, or even a sale or good deal on something because you didn't know someone in a position to tell you?

Have you ever helped someone because you had a relationship? Did you pass along their name or resume to a hiring manager? Did you recommend a class or a restaurant to a friend?

Did you survive a health crisis because friends and family supported you emotionally, mentally, and physically through it?

Do you see everyone in your life as a potential relationship of some kind, or do you limit your contact and relationship only to people you think might make you look good, or signal your status to others?

After hearing that story about the janitor, I often wonder how many of us have missed an opportunity because we didn't think someone else was worth listening to, or maybe didn't have anything to offer us, or we had nothing to offer them. He could have said, "I'm just the janitor. She won't listen to me," but he didn't.

What if this woman had simply taken the time to talk with him and been friendly, or acted professionally toward this man? Would the outcome have been different?

Do you act open to strangers, to students, to bus drivers, to random people you encounter daily regardless of their title, position, or personal or political beliefs?

I'm not saying we have to embrace everyone or disregard our intuition or safety, but who do you shun because they're "not enough" for some part of your image? Is it the Muslim if you're Christian, or the atheist if you're a believer of some kind? Can you have a positive relationship even if you disagree with someone? Do you assume you have nothing to offer others?

From childhood to adulthood, our relationships play a fundamental role in shaping who we are. They are multifaceted, comprising a range of psychological, social, and ethical elements. Ultimately, relationships not only impact our sense of self, but also serve as a cornerstone in our interactions with others.

Relationships are not only formative, they absolutely can be *transformative*. As children, our parents shape our well-being, or lack thereof, as well as our personalities and trajectories for learning, growth, and other relationships.

As teenagers, our friends, media, and/or community influence our behavior, proclivities, likes, and dislikes. Negative relationships can harm people for life. Positive relationships can catapult people to success and fulfillment. Whether we're aware of them or not, relationships impact nearly every aspect of life.

Positive relationships have been shown to help the outcome and survival of physical diseases (like breast cancer) and to cause sickness (like the number of scowls one partner gives to another can affect our immunity).[1]

Recent research indicates that positive and intimate relationships can change the gene expression and growth of tumors and protect against tumor growth.[2]

The other thing about relationships is that you can't predict the direction they'll take, or how people will step up to help you. Georgina, a seasoned and human-centered business strategist and consultant, experienced a very unique benefit of relationships: other mothers and women who stepped up to help her because they could and because she had nurtured her relationships with them in the past. She shares:

One time when my kid was young—way before Take Your Kid to Work Day, I had a babysitter that came to the house every morning. One morning, she called and said she couldn't come. She had a family emergency. I look at my kid, who wasn't even toilet trained. He was maybe two.

My husband had already left to go to work. I said, "Baby, we're going to get dressed and you have to come to work with me." We lived downtown and I worked out in Elk Grove Village. That commute was about an hour. The whole time he was in the back and I'm telling him, "You have to be good."

I had a meeting that morning, and my thinking was that if I could just do my meeting, then I would take the rest of the day off and we would go home.

The whole time, I'm like, "You've got to be good. You can't cry. You can't run around." We get to the parking lot and I give him another lecture. I had to sneak him in. First of all, this was when you weren't even supposed to have kids if you were in corporate management.

Secondly, if you did have kids, they didn't want to see them. That was an era when the guys would come and stand behind you at the Xerox machine to say, "How long are you going to be?" and they're leaning over you.

So, I sneak him up and asked my staff if he could just rotate from cube to cube during this meeting. They said they had it. I had a very good relationship with my team. I always had their back. They were single and when there was an assignment in Europe or South America, I would say, "You want to go to London next week?" I couldn't travel because I had a kid.

The women in the cafeteria were immigrant Caucasian women working in these manual labor jobs. Somehow, they heard that I had a kid upstairs on the second floor. They gathered up fruit, yogurt, crackers, and all of this food and sent it up with one of the staff. The staff got a conference room and put Marc in the conference room with all this food.

That's the value of relationships. I ended up staying because he was so quiet. We made it through the majority of the day with him understanding what he needed to do.

People started bringing little toys or objects they had in their desks for him to play with.

Eventually, my boss found out. He said, "I heard you have a visitor." He was cool about it though. I said, "Yeah, we're leaving now." We were there until about 3:00 p.m. Again, it's about being able to nurture all kinds of relationships. Respect people regardless of who you think they may be. We don't know until we sit down and we hear their story. You can't judge people by the way they look or act or the way they think you should be.

Positive relationships can enhance our well-being, foster our sense of identity, and promote our social and emotional development, while negative relationships can cause stress, anxiety, and even harm. And while many of us equate negative relationships with harmful or critical words, a negative relationship can be something as simple as an attitude. Loneliness or social isolation can have harmful effects on our bodies as well as our minds.

Positive effects of social relationships can be healing, including improved mental health, reduced stress, and increased resilience to stress. Social relationships can also provide us with a sense of purpose, belonging, and social support, which can be protective against negative health outcomes. These effects are direct and indirect. For example, behaviors can be contagious. People may be more likely to engage in healthy behaviors, such as regular exercise, if their community or friends are doing so.

Negative effects of social relationships include increased risk of depression, anxiety, and substance abuse, as well as greater risk of mortality. Negative social interactions such as conflict or lack of support can lead to feelings of loneliness, isolation, and distress, which in turn can contribute to negative health outcomes.

For example, individuals who lack social support may have a harder time managing chronic illnesses, such as diabetes or heart disease, which can lead to poorer health outcomes.

Georgina expressed that her relationships within her family and the encompassing sociopolitical milieu, exerted both positive and negative influences on her. Nevertheless, she realized that associations with others inherently come with their own advantages and disadvantages:

> My family history was one of bondage in the South. People really didn't talk about it. On my mother's side, my family came from urban South Carolina, and they took pride in saying that one of my great, great relatives was the cook for the governor.

> That meant that person was in the "big house" and they somehow believed that they were better off than those people who were forced to work in the field. That was all we heard about that side of the family.

> My dad was from rural Mississippi. When I say rural, I mean, it was totally rural. In fact, just a few years ago we went to a funeral for a cousin and the GPS (Global Positioning System) got us to a certain point and then stopped.

> We were in the middle of a dirt road at a clearing. Do we go left? Do we go right? We called another cousin and told them we were lost and he said, "Where are you?" We said, "We don't know." He said, "What do you see?" I said, "There's a tree that's kind of bending over." He said, "I know where you are. I'll be there. I'll come and get you." About 15 minutes later, he shows up and escorts us. As I said, it was rural.

The Importance of Relationships on Every Level

My father's family didn't talk much about what their experiences were other than the fact he had 10 siblings. His grandparents had a lot of siblings as well. During the slave era, there was a brother who somehow got separated and was then eventually lost.

The family originated in the Carolinas via West Africa and the triangle trade routes, then Georgia and somehow ended up in Mississippi. Somebody was sold off to a son or daughter and they went westward.

They had a very rural existence even after the Civil War. My grandmother remained on the farm until she passed away.

That was my father's side. All eleven children are deceased. Their descendants are spread throughout the United States. However, a few cousins and their offspring still live in rural Mississippi. There are no one farms for a living anymore. It's forest land at this point.

After World War II my dad came up to Chicago because he had an uncle residing in Bronzeville. My dad was in one of the segregated all-Black tank battalions stationed in the UK and France during the war. When those Black soldiers arrived in the villages to secure the fronts, the people of Britain and France were so glad to see American troops, they didn't care whether they were Black or what.

They opened their homes and fed them because they had been living in the tanks. They allowed them to take baths and took care of them. Then, once they secured that front, then the Army sent in air support and other soldiers and sent the tank battalion on to the next front.

When these black soldiers were on the train coming back to the South after the war, he said when they got to Maryland, the train stopped, and all the Black soldiers had to give up their seats.

They had to go to one of the storage/cattle cars because of Jim Crow laws that existed in the South.

They had German prisoners of war that they were also carrying down to military bases and they had to give up their seats in Maryland for the German prisoners of war.

When he got back to Mississippi, they were calling him "boy" and all this and he said no. His mom gathered enough money for him to get on a bus and come to Chicago. That's how he met my mom. Her family had relocated from the Carolinas to Chicago.

That's all we know. We still have family land in Mississippi so we're able to get together as cousins and work through what that means for the family as a whole. It helps us in terms of having reunions and being able to talk to one another and lay the foundation for future generations to continue to connect and support each other.

Her story speaks to the sociopolitical conditions of her childhood, her coming of age, and her adulthood. Georgina's family history and how she was reared is both a representation of a larger Black oppressed experience as well one of victory. Despite the deleterious relationship between her family and the surrounding society, her family's internal relationships created resilience and allowed for Georgina, the executive, consultant, social leader, and thoughtful change maker, to emerge. Here Georgina shares more about the path she took:

Relationships as Resilience

Once I had to stand in for Valerie Jarrett. This was before she became the Valerie Jarrett that everyone knows. She was supposed to give a workshop at the Women in Transportation Conference. At the time, she was with the Chicago Transit Authority and was the CEO. At the last minute, she was called away to do something, and her chief of staff, who I had met once before, called me and said, "Would you mind standing in for Ms. Jarrett? She's not able to do it." I said sure.

I go into this session and it's a room full of all kinds of women who work in transportation all over the country. They were there to learn how to be mentored. My thing at the time was not so much about finding a mentor because they were in transportation, a very male-dominated industry. I came from a career in transportation. You can spend your life in the company looking for someone to lift you up. What happens if that person gets transferred, retires, or gets fired, and you've been depending on this one individual to boost you up in the organization versus being in a position where you can reach beneath you and build your infantry of people that can push you up. Then, when you have vacancies in your department, you don't have to recruit someone else's team member. You have your own tribe to draw from. When your boss sees that you have a group of people that are supporting you and championing your efforts and you're able to build your work team with people that embrace you, understand you, and recognize that you are their chief supporter, the sky is the limit for how you move up in that organization. Even if you decide to move to another organization, you have people you can bring with you.

As women, we're always believing that we can find some white male or some other male or woman that somehow has gotten a notch ahead of us, be the lining of their coattail, versus exercising our own leadership and bringing other people along.

If I could impart that wisdom by any means necessary and understand that we are smart, we are bright, we are kind, we can be considerate, and we should always be visionary. We always have to look beyond the obvious and don't accept the status quo if it's not working for you and your village.

Georgina has shown how we're able to lift ourselves and each other up in this unjust system through our relationships. I like her story because it demonstrates how relationships are a tool for changing our society. I like how she's shown that relationships are not just about connection between people but *about the benefits to each person in the relationship.*

For instance, there's a large, flowering bush called a peony that is very popular around the country. People who aren't familiar with the flower will try to kill the swarms of ants that appear as soon as the flower begins to bloom in the spring. What many don't realize is that the peony's flowers provide food for the ants, and the ants, in turn, protect the flowers from other floral-feeding insects. It's called mutualism, a relationship in which two organisms of different species benefit from the activity of one another.[3]

Mutualism is a type of symbiotic relationship where all species involved benefit from their interactions. There are two kinds of mutualism. In some cases, the species are entirely dependent on each other (obligate mutualism), and in others, they derive benefits from their relationship but could survive without each other (facultative mutualism)."[4]

Bees that pollinate flowers and various plants are a common example of facultative mutualism, as is Georgina's example of the Black woman executive and the janitor. Although the executive declined a friendly, casual, relationship, the potential of what was there is an excellent example of how different positions or groups of people could benefit each other—had the woman been open to the opportunity.

Our survival as individuals, a community, and a species—and as leaders—depends on our relationships with those around us, and I don't just mean our peers. Those strangers who make decisions about the laws and policies that affect our day-to-day lives, those we pass on our way to work or school, those who pick the vegetables and fruit we eat or take our card as we pay for clothes—all of these relationships affect us in profound and sometimes subtle yet substantial ways. Intentionally deepening into relationships is part of the path to our liberation. We should remember that no matter the distance, "I am you, you are me." As we connect more authentically and step into our mutuality, we can all transcend.

Chapter 5: The Importance of Relationships

1. How do your relationships reflect your values and support your needs?
2. In a tech-driven world, how do you balance personal connections with professional growth?

Georgina Heard-Labonne

Georgina Heard-Labonne (she/her) is a seasoned strategic executive with an extensive transportation management, government, business, and community leadership background.

She currently works for a Chicago-based management practice, optimizing government, people, and community organizing wellness summits, town halls, and B2B expos. While at the Illinois Department of Transportation, she supported freight rail infrastructure investment in Chicago. She also ensured compliance with new federal Public Transit Rail Safety mandates.

As a United Airlines' registered lobbyist, Georgina led external affairs in Washington, DC and the Midwest before and after 9/11. At United's human resources department, she created the company's first global management succession plan and benefits center. Her diversity, equity, and inclusion initiatives were cited by President Bill Clinton and featured in a Harvard Business School case study.

Collaborating with the White House and the City of Chicago, she facilitated business leaders in welfare reform by requesting

expanded workforce policies for former welfare recipients. Her approach won her prominent appointments on the Chicago Workforce Board, Illinois Governor's Immigration Reform Task Force, and the Illinois Housing Task Force. She also spoke at various leadership conferences and served on President Barack Obama's USDOT TRACS Committee for Transit Rail Safety.

Georgina holds a master's in clinical psychology from DePaul University and a psychology degree from Bradley University. She trained under the renowned Jay Haley at the Institute of Family Therapy. She enjoys art, photography, travel, and music in her free time. Georgina is a member of The Links, Incorporated, and lives in Chicago and Las Vegas with her family.

Chapter 6
The Role of Mentors and Relationships in Professional and Leadership Development

Mentors are like butterflies. Caterpillars go through a transition where they turn into butterflies. Because of their transitional journey, they obtain the perspective of the life of a caterpillar and what it's like to fly. They have a larger perspective and can see the entire forest. They can see there's pollen over here, and it's all leafy greens over there. We need to bring this pollen over there so that place can experience the colors that we are able to see over here. They have a full perspective.

— Nicole Wilson

Stafford Hood, PhD

I first met Dr. Stafford Hood while interviewing for the counseling psychology doctoral program at Arizona State University. I'd read about him and his work while preparing for my interview.

Through his scholarly work, he introduced me to his struggle as a Black evaluator, the socially critical analysis he often exercised when viewing the field and his experience, and his lifelong curiosity and intellectual adventurousness.

Then, I had the life-changing opportunity to match the words and essence with his face and presence. After my interview with him, he called me and said that even if I did not choose to attend Arizona State University, I could still reach out to him for support. That one small moment was an example of the level of compassion and scaffolding he gave to me and so many others.

I eventually chose to attend Arizona State University, mostly because of Stafford. He became my advisor, teacher, and mentor. He guided me through learning about evaluation, honing skills in culturally responsive evaluation (CRE), and conducting my first evaluation—an international evaluation in Tanzania.

The Role of Mentorships and Relationships in Professional and Leadership Development

"When you enter a new town or neighborhood," Stafford told me, "go to the local bar, sit with the people, and talk." The bars, churches, and other gatherings I chose often involved music, one of Stafford's other passions. The people there were, well, just people. They had their own histories, stories, and opinions, and most were not shy about sharing them. I wasn't shy about listening.

I'd later come to know how much jazz, in particular (Stafford's favorite), was a background (and foreground) for what I was about to discover about history, evaluation, and community—the kinds of things I couldn't learn in a classroom.

Through his guidance, I learned the unwritten as well as the written laws of evaluation. Stafford not only taught tangible evaluation skills, like developing relevant evaluation questions and designing data collection methods. He also instilled the values of building relationships with the people who were most impacted by the evaluation and how to experience the participants' contexts directly.

For more than three decades, Stafford schooled his students in the kind of history that was absent in our formal training. Using his own experience, stories, and race, he elevated the contributions of African Americans. He didn't just teach social justice—he gave it context, flavor, and meaning juxtaposing it against a historical backdrop of exploitation and oppression, strength, and resilience.

Stafford created the Nobody Knows My Name project, which raised up distinguished African American evaluator scholars whose work was eclipsed and ignored by their White counterparts.

He led by example. He taught me that we can never truly lead or teach culture until we know history—a concept that greatly influenced my worldview today.

He passed away suddenly in January 2023, but left behind a legacy that exceeded his professorship. He helped many of us go far beyond the classroom when it came to thinking about the meaning and role of culture, cultural responsibility, and relationships in our own lives and work. He taught me that all of us can become mentors, coaches, and leaders.

Stafford's mentorship taught me that relationships matter—both the relationships we have with communities, friends, and family, as well as the ones we have in the form of mentors. Call these wise men and women coaches, leaders, or mentors, they often do elevate us to success and help us achieve our dreams.

If parents hold a unique and special place in our lives, then so do our mentors. They pick up where our parents leave off, teaching us the things we need to know as young adults, and older adults and leaders.

They are pivotal in getting certain positions, navigating environments, and learning the dos and don'ts of leadership, an organization, or discipline. They teach us to network, to listen, and to engage with others. Those are the critical things we learn from mentors.

Being a mentor is a challenge and a learning experience as well. A mentor's role is to provide guidance, advice, feedback, and support to the mentee. As Stafford demonstrated so well, a mentor also serves as a role model, teacher, counselor, advisor, sponsor, advocate, and ally.

Mentors don't force change on their mentees, or mold them into mini-versions of themselves. They provide their mentees with the tools, relationships, coaching, and guidance they need to become a better version of themselves.

Our supervisors, managers, teachers, and others mentor us, but our first mentors, our first coaches are very often our parents, our siblings, and our peers. It all matters. Who are you mentoring? Who has mentored you? What have you learned? What are you learning? What do you want to learn?

Nicole Wilson created mentors where she couldn't find them and found them in relationships where mentorship wasn't necessarily the goal:

> I wholeheartedly go into some relationships saying, "I want to be mentored by this person," and the person has not necessarily accepted that role. But I will keep pretending that this person is my mentor. It's worked out.
>
> I've yet to come against somebody that I wanted to be mentored by and that person has pushed me away.

Nicole, a young, burgeoning impact leader, is one of eight girls, raised in the Bronzeville neighborhood of Chicago by a mother who was in foster care herself. As she shares:

> To give us opportunities she didn't have, my mom worked hard to provide us with music lessons and ballet, even traveling far for classes.
>
> My mom knew me. I didn't even know that she knew me at a deep level. We experienced homelessness and had to live with our aunt for a few months during the first quarter of a school year. It was my first time ever being away from my mom.
>
> When we went back with my mom after that, I behaved differently. I responded in crazy ways. I was cursing out teachers, throwing things. Insane ways that my fourth-grade self responded to that. Eventually, we got back on the straight and narrow. When I was 20, my sisters and I were sitting in the living room, and somebody brought up how me and my mom's relationship wasn't close at that time.
>
> With most kids, you're super close to your parents when you're younger, then your teen years hit and you're separated. By the time my siblings were 20, they were back being closer to my mom. I wasn't.
>
> We were talking about it, but I couldn't put into words why until my mom said, "She's never forgiven me for not being with her." I thought, "What?" I was blown away by that one, she knew that. I was also blown away realizing that that was the reason that held me from being intimately close to her again.
>
> She didn't hold it against me. It blew my mind that she could pinpoint exactly when our relationship changed. From then, I was able to talk to her about things. It blew my mind how much my mom knew. She knew us like no one else.
>
> I didn't even know that was the reason, but she knew. Think about moms and their infinite wisdom. She showed her wisdom.

I'm so grateful that we had that family conversation because I was 20, and she passed when I was 32. For the last 10 years, we were able to have that close relationship again.

I felt like she would have pressed for it a little more, but she let me come back in my own time. The amount of wisdom and insight that she had into all of us was crazy. She didn't hold it against me, and she didn't plead her own case. When I got older, I understood. She physically had no place for me to be with her at that time. But she never tried to plead her own case and say, "I did this for you." No, she took the brunt of all our angst. The amount of grace that took. She never held it against any of us.

Nicole's mother gracefully exemplified the qualities of a remarkable mentor: patience, empathy, understanding, selflessness, and unwavering dedication. This nurturing experience fostered a mindset of receptiveness, inspiring her to seek mentorship from others.

Many of us either don't think we need mentors, don't know where or how to access them, or don't see opportunities to be mentored. Through our evaluation work, many women express the power mentorship and coaching have in their leadership journey. It teaches us, uplifts us, and supports us. Mentorship shows up in cultures across the world, in teaching people how to survive, gain new skills, or even rear children. However, in an individualistic and socially separated context like the US, the pervasiveness of mentorship possibilities can get clouded.

Here, starting with a community mindset can send us in the right direction. As Nicole adds:

I was fortunate to attend a predominantly Black school in Bronzeville in the '90s, with mostly Black teachers.

It was extremely important when we experienced homelessness. It was extremely important when we had to live with our dad for the first time. All of us behaved differently and responded differently to that.

Even though I acted out, I was only suspended once. It never damaged my trajectory in school.

The Black women and men in that school, unknowingly showing us the grace that we needed, were our mentors. I wasn't labeled as a child with behavioral problems, and I wholeheartedly know that was because of the community that was built around, not just my family, but that neighborhood. The school was predominantly four or five major families. Everyone knew everyone. Even for us, my older cousins went to that school. We had a lineage. We had care across community. If I did something, somebody was going to tell my mom. We didn't know it at the time, but it was unique.

That has shaped my view of the educational system today. I'm very passionate about the preservation of community in schools because we drastically went away from that. We have pulled away from even family nights in schools. That's nearly unheard of now where I grew up.

That sense of community has deeply influenced what I do now —working for University of Chicago's crime lab and education lab.

What they're trying to create is something that is very dear to me —that community, that full 360-degree reach. It wasn't just the school population. It wasn't just one institution, it was the entirety of all of these different actors and stakeholders advocating for the collective growth of the students and kids there at the time.

I feel completely able to be taken care of. I feel that I can do the same for everybody else in that community. My purpose is to help people find their group of people like that, whether it be in an organization or their own family that they built. It's to help them find exactly what that looks like in their community.

I'm opposed to this individualistic mentality. It's detrimental to our way of life. It's not how we were meant to live. When I hear people say, "You can cut that person off," or "You can do this by yourself," I tell them I've done nothing by myself. I've done nothing without community. And I don't want to.

A lot of people come from a place of hurt where "this community does this." That wasn't your community. You have to find your community as opposed to saying that you don't need community. We all do.

Mentors and Coaches

People sometimes get mentoring, coaching, and friendships confused. All three relationships have some form of guidance and support, but they differ in several key aspects, like the focus, structure, and nature of the relationship.

Mentoring, for instance, focuses primarily on the personal and professional development of the mentee. The mentor shares their knowledge, experiences, and wisdom to guide and support the mentee's growth and development in a specific field or area, like Stafford did with me and his other students. Like Stafford, mentors are typically people with significant experience and expertise in a particular domain. They draw upon their knowledge, experience, lessons learned, and insights to guide and advise their mentee.

Mentoring relationships tend to be more casual, informal, and longer-term. Mentors often have a deeper, ongoing relationship with their mentees, providing ongoing support, advice, and guidance over an extended period. Of course, some mentorships can be short and for one specific challenge.

In general, mentoring relationships are more personal and have a deeper, more supportive connection between the mentor and mentee, sometimes providing emotional support and guidance based on their own experiences.

Coaching primarily focuses on achieving specific goals and improving a person's performance by helping the coachee identify their strengths, challenges, and goals. A coach provides guidance and strategies to enhance a person's skills. Many times, they work with people at the intersection of goal achievement and skill development. Coaching relationships are typically more structured and shorter-term and tend to involve a specific number of sessions or a defined timeline.

Coaches are often skilled in the coaching process and techniques rather than necessarily being subject matter experts. They help those being coached explore their own potential, unlock their abilities, and facilitate self-discovery and self-improvement.

Coaching relationships are typically more objective and focused on the coachee's development. Coaches ask thought-provoking questions, challenge assumptions, and help the coachee gain clarity and take ownership of their growth.

Overall, mentoring tends to have a broader focus on holistic development and longer-term relationships, while coaching is more goal-oriented and focused on specific outcomes.

Both mentoring and coaching have unique benefits and can be valuable in different contexts. Some of our earliest mentors and coaches are teachers, as are our most memorable ones. Nicole explains:

> I had an amazing teacher in first grade. She stuck with us from first grade through third grade. What I took from her is the crucial importance of if you're getting mentored, it is your responsibility to mentor.

She gave me a presence outside of the home of somebody that was invested and cared about my success and individual growth. I wanted to be seen as an individual. I didn't want to be seen as just one of eight. Although I was in first grade, I still had never seen that. She invested in me in a way that was very evident.

She stuck with our class because she fell in love with our class. She fell in love with who we were individually. She wanted to see us progress and stuck with us as long as she could.

I'm dyslexic so my spelling was horrible in grade school. I cannot identify sounds with letters. It just does not work in my brain. I remember doing spelling tests and she would religiously take the time out to go through the words with me.

Other students got reprimanded when they didn't do great. I never was reprimanded. She took the time out to invest in me in the areas in which she knew I was behind my peers. That's not something she did with anyone else.

Out of this nascent experience grew a thirst for mentorship. Mentorship can show up expectedly or unexpectedly, in areas of education, professional development, personal growth, or everyday interactions. We must be ready for these spontaneous opportunities as well as intentional in seeking out guidance. Nicole shares further:

For mentorship to be effective, to work well, it's important to be open to any relationship becoming a mentoring relationship but also situating yourself in a place where you can always be mentored. I can sometimes do that without knowing. To do that, I think you have to be aware of who is around you and be aware of where relationships can take you. It can turn into a mentoring relationship at any point.

I can think of a few that drastically changed my life. One was my mentor at CPS [Chicago Public Schools]. She was over the student adjudication department. She changed the way the district disciplined kids. Her message and structure went to all of the schools that you can't just expel these kids. You can't just say, "I don't want this kid in the school anymore." It has to be an expellable offense.

I tremendously loved her for showing me this alternative to the way we think about a school district like CPS. In this small way, you can make an effective change. It affected hundreds of students' lives every year. She had to fight for it and go toe to toe with a lot of people about it, but it made a difference. I was tremendously impacted by her and her mentorship and learned about how important it is to get the right stakeholders in the room.

Another one of my mentors is a professor at Benedictine. She helped me get into the University of Chicago. She helped me to understand the importance of the educational significance of UChicago including the way that I would be able to speak a different language when I would go into these difference sectors. I wasn't interested in going to UChicago at all. I did not want to go. Growing up, the interactions with the university left a bad taste. I didn't want to be anywhere around UChicago. She helped me understand the connections of the alumni that have been a part of the university and introduced me to some phenomenal people that are very like-minded that are part of the alumni pool. Then she advocated for me.

Another mentor came when I was in college and I didn't know what I wanted to do. This woman worked at the mayor's office. I applied for this position at the mayor's office. Everyone was clambering for this position. She gave me a chance, but she didn't let me feel or let me know that it was a chance. "You're here. You're supposed to be here. You're meant to be here." She gave me work that I felt was above my skills, but she helped me to meet those goals. She allowed me to grow.

My last supervisor was a White woman. I knew it would be different, but you can be surprised who can be a mentor if you're open to it. I'm grateful that I went into the experience and relationship with the notion of a clean slate. I was surprised at how she has mentored me professionally *and* personally. She has given me challenges professionally and then checked in on a human level.

In some ways, Nicole is a master mentee and now growing into a master mentor from all the rich mentorship she's received as a child and adult. As she adds:

When I was in college, I mentored at the school that I used to go to. They paired us with a student. I took her to my college and around the city. It didn't seem like she was interested in anything we discussed or saw.

She was in seventh grade. On the last day of our mentoring sessions, there was a big celebration at the school. I came with some flowers and a gift card.

I'm so grateful that one of my old teachers was still there. I went to say hi and she said, "Nicole, I've been hearing about you from Beyonce. She is so enamored. You've helped her come out of her shell here."

She hadn't given me any feedback, but she was a bright light at school and talked about everything we did. I wanted something, but I didn't. I wanted her to soak it all in and take it back. It wasn't meant for me. It was meant for her to use it in her classrooms. It was meant for the green fields.

It is your responsibility if you are being mentored to mentor others. I stand by this idea that if liberation is to happen, we all have to be teachers. Whether we are teaching the oppressed or the oppressor, we are all a part of teaching and we have something to teach.

Chapter 6: Mentorship and Leadership Development

1. What have you gained from mentors, and what could you benefit from now?
2. What is your mentorship superpower, and how can you use it to guide others?

Nicole Wilson

Nicole Wilson (she/her) is a driven and talented leader currently serving as the data and compliance manager at UChicago Urban Labs. She graduated with distinction from Roosevelt University, earning her bachelor of science in business administration. Her passion for better communities led her to pursue a master's in public policy and management at the University of Chicago Harris School of Public Policy.

Nicole has become an essential part of the Urban Labs team with her deep expertise in nonprofit organizations, program evaluation, program development, staff development, and community outreach. Her dedication, work ethic, and exceptional managerial skills have tremendously impacted the organization's success. She spearheads the data and compliance department, ensuring the organization meets ethical and government regulations standards. She also leads the development and implementation of various programs that have benefited numerous communities in Chicago.

Nicole's commitment to community outreach goes beyond her work at Urban Labs. She has volunteered with several local charities, which reflects her strong sense of civic responsibility. She brings significant strength to the Urban Labs team and the community.

Chapter 7
Relationship-Building Practices for Organizations

My mom is a big Barbra Streisand fan. We watched old and new movies of hers growing up. One movie—*Funny Girl*—struck me uniquely because of the song "People." This idea of "people who need people are the luckiest people in the world" is against the reigning paradigm in the US. With significant inner work, I came to cherish this sentiment and now lean into it in work, growth, and play.

Creating an organization conducive to relationship building is more about creating an emotional and psychological space, as we practice at BECOME.

We create space for relationship building in check-ins, greetings, questions, and presence with each other. We ask questions like, how are you arriving? What's inspiring you? What's bringing you joy? What's on your heart lately?

And then we encourage relationships. We encourage people to connect one-on-one to have lunch together. We have a very supportive environment.

If somebody is going through something, the team is there, like when my mentor, Dr. Stafford Hood, died earlier this year. I felt embraced by the team during that time. They stepped up to help but gave me room and support to grieve. We offer and create space to heal, gather, support each other, coach, and mentor. We explicitly call for and practice authenticity and vulnerability, even though we may not get it right every time.

At BECOME, we are committed to fostering a space and an organization that values and uplifts relationships—that is an antidote to the toxicity of exaggerated competition and individualism.

Tatiana Cortes, a human and relationship-centered leader at BECOME, exemplifies what it means to be in strong relationship with others. They are one of the many people who has used the space at BECOME to grow, change, and uplift others:

> I identify as a first-generation Afro-Latinx American. My mom is from Puerto Rico and my dad is from Colombia, but I was born and raised in Roxbury in Boston. I also identify as queer and non-binary and believe we all should figure out what it means to have a balance of both of those things and move away from disparate constructs of feminine and masculine, while recognizing that we all have the ability to channel both of them.

> What drew me to BECOME is that people aren't here just as a place to work. They feel like this work is part of our shared community.

> There is a feeling that BECOME is willing to question itself, receive feedback, and say that we're not perfect and do not have it right every time.

> I really appreciate that we are an organization that's really moving away from being an organization of hierarchy. Our titles mean nothing. Our status means nothing.

> Relationships are important. Relationships of trust are important. That looks different for each person in what they consider

are important contexts in relationships. We are in a process of learning and growing in this area as an organization.

For me, consent is important. Wanting to know people's boundaries and agreements are important. Wanting to know how people like to work and be in better relationships is really important to me. I try to hold that in any space where I'm working with people and doing work with them.

The other thing that makes BECOME a healing space is that there's an acknowledgment around systems—both as individuals and as an organization—of how we are all impacted by systems, mainly oppressive and racial caste systems.

One of the things I love best is that we're all leaders, no matter what position we hold. What has been supportive to me in my own self-development is when I know I'm in a relationship with someone else who doesn't see me as less than as a human or a person. It's supportive when I'm in a relationship with someone who is able to hold the contradictions and complexities of what it means to be a human and who can honor being messy and being imperfect.

Each of us is willing to go on a journey of self-exploration within our work. We support each other with compassion and vulnerability to grow. With BECOME, boldness and innovation are the norm. We experiment with what it means to have an organization that embodies our mission and values. We're moving towards a non-hierarchical structure and there's a focus on achieving excellence while also taking care of ourselves. It becomes challenging when conflict arises but I believe this is something all people in organizations are trying to figure out.

At the organizational level, we're implementing sociocracy, which is intended to create collective systems and processes that further foster safety and productivity. It, along with other intentions, will enhance our internal processes and external practices by prioritizing relationships, trust, and communication.

Through our journey as an organization, we have learned many lessons about relationships and beyond.

Creating time and space for human-to-human connections is key for fostering strong relationships within organizations and spaces. This can mean setting aside a weekly meeting or dedicated gathering for fun or wellness. Encouraging collaboration and co-creation through team structures and partnerships further enhances these connections.

Spaces that cater to various aspects of interpersonal relationships, such as professional development, personal growth, peer-to-peer coaching, and unbridled fun, all aim at creating a space for human connection and bonding. This quintessential approach to relationships acknowledges the multi-faceted nature of human beings and our connections, resulting in a living, breathing organism that thrives on the complexities of human interaction.

Acknowledging the intricacy of our relationships ignites their vibrance. My teammates, whom I connect with through work, purpose, and friendship, exemplify this truth. Often people advocate for compartmentalizing work and pleasure. But embracing structure and principles while acknowledging our multifaceted bonds allows their full potential to unfold.

Limiting relationships to a binary framework deprives them of their richness. We must exercise discernment and wisdom for our relationships to thrive. By doing so, our connections will continue to flourish and nourish every aspect of our lives.

Spaces that welcome emotions and emotional intelligence recognize that emotions are often the drivers of our micro-to-macro expressions, decisions, and proclivities. Though we may not always be conscious of it, emotions guide us in every moment.

When we intentionally create space for emotions, we invite our fully human selves into the room.

This intentional approach to emotions can be as simple as asking how someone is feeling or a more in-depth conversation around life experiences and meaning-making. Leaders who prioritize both social and emotional intelligence can create spaces that support deeper social connections through check-ins and one-on-one relationship building. In my experience with BECOME, many teammates became my closest allies and purpose partners. They function as friends and family in how they celebrate my successes and support me through painful experiences.

By inviting emotions into our spaces, we intentionally embrace our humanity, bringing greater authenticity to our decision making and relationships.

Social intelligence encompasses more than just good relationships. It involves empathy on deep levels and moving in unity with others when appropriate. It's understanding that cultivating relationships feeds into overall well-being holistically.

Language is also a powerful tool in creating cohesion, and collation is at the heart of language: we, us, together, co-creating. Even though I strive for a consistent collective voice, I find myself using *I, my, I did* too frequently. It's easy to overlook the influence and impact others have on our successes, experiences, or growth. Simply put, we need each other to grow and to thrive. In essence, *we* are not complete without each other.

When we use the language of the collective, we acknowledge the work and energy of others and how that influences us and the outcome. Words also create, so when we use "we", we breathe into the collective and move towards unity and authenticity. Let's look at some of the skills and characteristics of a leader that supports authentic connections.

Authenticity and genuine expression. When we express ourselves from our hearts and say our truths, we can not only be seen by others for who we truly are, but we also welcome others to be their authentic selves.

I used to think that saying what I truly thought would push others away. When I allowed fear to hinder my expression, it pushed people away because they didn't know my true thoughts, and my silence created chasms between us. We couldn't move together because my lack of authenticity slowed us down. Through generative and constructive conflict with others, driven by love and truth, I've pushed through fears and genuinely connected with my teammates. This authenticity and connection has fueled efficiency and fulfillment at work and in my relationships.

Communication. Leaders have to be able to communicate on multiple levels. The majority of communication takes place outside of words. It's the nonverbals, facial expressions, body movements (or lack of), and body positions. It's the tone of voice. Thus, for healthy relationships, we need to be able to communicate holistically with teams, neighbors, and those we're serving or in partnership with.

Facilitating synergy. Facilitation is an amazing skill set when done well. It allows someone to guide a group through change, co-creation, or unity. A group can progress, heal, and create together through this process. A good facilitator uplifts a relationship-centered space to places that a group may have never thought it could go. For example, we hold visioning sessions with other people in organizations and communities. People often come in fixated on a problem but they leave more connected to the people in the room, hopeful, and visionary. Facilitation can transform.

Seeing interdependencies and potential connections between people. Many times, we (people) can see things in people that they don't see in themselves or others. It's part of being human. None of us can see everything. This is why we need each other—to see the whole picture and the truth.

A leader can cultivate this vision, to see potential in others as well as see ways people's strengths can complement each other to uplift and complete the whole. Learning to mediate restorative conflicts is one of the most challenging skills for me. I used to avoid confrontation, but the leaders I work with have taught me and pushed me to confront conflict and find potential and beauty in it.

Friction is the essence of life. It's a concept that reminds me of "Under Pressure" by David Bowie and Queen. The track implies that our reality creates friction, and it's only by embracing it that we can exist. Therefore, we need to lean into it and love the beauty of confronting conflicts.

Emotional and social intelligence are crucial for positive work relationships. Fostering these skills in employees or teammates can be accomplished by implementing training and coaching.

In a work setting, evaluating performance and developing leadership programs that incorporate these qualities can promote a positive work environment, enhance leadership effectiveness and team performance, and improve well-being. In a living space like a block or neighborhood, uplifting the language and importance of relationships and social and emotional intelligence can steer a group towards each other.

Tatiana has learned and contributed so many lessons in relationship building that they've drawn from their childhood and hone and build in their adulthood. As Tatiana offers:

> As I've gotten older, I see how I was molded by my community. My community felt like one of care. My parents knew other kids'

parents and other kids. There was a feeling of looking out for each other and being connected and supported. It was a sense that all children are everyone's children.

My sense of purpose has evolved as I have continued to evolve. At first, I believed my purpose was supporting other people to find their own voice. This came out of my community in Boston, supporting me to find my own voice. This made me realize that people don't need help finding their own voices, but that people have their own voices and are not given the spaces, and are not always intentionally heard.

I'm really interested in relationships. There are way more liberatory ways that we can engage in relationships. I see my purpose connected to how I, through being my most authentic self in any given moment, propel other people to move towards liberatory relationships.

Relationships need trust. That's a word that's thrown around a lot, but it takes time and looks different for each person.

Relationships take work. I personally believe that every person has a story or stories to be told. That process is a vulnerable process for people to engage in and it's not often welcomed in spaces outside of partnerships, outside of our homes. But when we tell our stories and listen to others', we can transform together.

Chapter 7: Relationship-Building Practices for Organizations

1. In cultures that prioritize individualism, how can relationships take center stage?
2. How can you facilitate deeper connections within your community or organization?

Tatiana Cortes

Tatiana Cortes (she/they) is a civic and cultural organizer who values advancing racial equity and is committed to social work, art, and justice among LGBTQ+ and BIPOC communities.

Tatiana has benefited from the support of social service systems and communities of care. They believe that when policies, systems, and behaviors are rooted in care for everyone, all of society will thrive. Tatiana loves Chicago and the long-standing tradition of striving to make the city more equitable for everybody.

Tatiana has a background in philanthropy, community organizing, public policy, and nonprofits. These diverse experiences have equipped them to think on their feet when analyzing situations, reimagining solutions, and changing course to create and sustain relationships, gather and share essential resources, and establish community-informed and driven priorities.

As the child of two deaf parents and a sibling to a younger brother, Tatiana learned to listen before speaking, observe at the margins, and advocate for resources. From studying theology and sociology to pursuing a master's in social work policy, Tatiana brings many experiences that trained them to seek and hold complexities.

As a practitioner, Tatiana is enthusiastic about planting and watering seeds for individual and communal growth. They believe our problems are all of ours, and we can have humanistic relationships, institutions, and societies.

Their leadership through BECOME has grown and fostered relationships with the community and cultivated collective healing towards transformation.

Section Three

Intersectionality: Exploring One's Cultural Mosaic

Each of us comes with a variety of cultural, historical, and ethnic influences that shape our identity, how we show up in the world, and how we're perceived and treated.

As leaders, especially WOC, we can find such richness in exploring our cultural mosaic, our intersectionality. We must also know culture and intersectionality as they deeply affect how we navigate and, at times, are able to navigate the world given fabricated barriers people and structures can pose.

Community is composed of various cultural groups, each contributing to the overall richness and uniqueness of the collective culture. Exploring one's cultural mosaic involves actively engaging with and learning about the diverse cultural elements present in not only our own culture, and community, but in the society outside of our own.

This section celebrates and cautions us to go deeper in this exploration.

Chapter 8
The What and Why of Intersectionality

My then five-year-old daughter came home from school one day and asked why someone had killed Martin Luther King, Jr., and why people were treated badly because of the color of their skin. At that moment, I stopped breathing.

In hopes of protecting my daughter from premature pain and decontextualized trauma, I had been trying to postpone this conversation for as long as I could. It may seem ironic, as a social justice advocate and someone who teaches adults about structural oppression and equity, that I'd be without words at this moment. But, given my own intersectionality, it may make more sense.

My assumption as a mother of a kindergartener was that she wasn't quite ready to understand the complexity of human oppression. I didn't think she would be able to not take it personally that she is a girl of color in a nation that paints a grim and hopeless picture of people who look like us.

I feared all past and future possibilities coming true. Growing up in a majority White town and being the focus of racial slurs and oppressive heartbreak, the deeply personal and simultaneous macro struggle crushed my voice in that moment.

My intersectionality traversed time and space and momentarily paralyzed me. As a mother, I wanted to protect her from any kind of pain and heartache. As a Black woman, I saw myself in her, the little Black girl growing up in a world of rejection. As a social justice advocate, the anger swelled as the outside world creeped into the interstices of family life.

As a psychologist, thoughts of Kenneth and Mamie Clark's doll test (pictures of little Black children choosing White dolls when given the option of the Black or White one being the "nice doll.") knocked into the walls of my mind, reverberating so loudly, I could barely hear any wisdom underneath.

It took me a couple moments to clear the clutter of the past, present, and potential future to speak to my daughter.

Grabbing for some semblance of clarity, concreteness, and compassion, I told her that Martin Luther King, Jr. fought for people and for love. I told her that people who are taught the wrong thing or are hurt by others can act out of their pain and hurt other people, and it's wrong to hurt others for any reason. And more importantly, I told her that I love her.

As she grows up and is able to understand the complexity of inter-sectionality I'll share the history of her great-grandfather with her —how he helped lead Haitians to safety during the politically turbulent and violent times, risking his life and family to help others.

I'll tell her about things that may make her angry, or make her question her own experience, or challenge her own detractors. That's how she'll grow into her own power, through critical thinking, observation, and experience, and with compassion.

Intersectionality affects every single one of us, but it affects each of us differently. If we change one identity ingredient from this mix, we get a very different result. Let's take ethnicity. If I were, instead, a White woman, leaving all other aspects the same, my physical, emotional, and mental reaction and experience would be completely different.

The pain associated with the past or the depth of anger would be weaker or even disappear completely. There would likely be a disconnect with how personal a past figure like Dr. King is to me.

The fear around the impact of this history, story, and reality would dissipate and I might even treat this as a teachable moment (if I were an ally or co-conspirator), at best. Instead of ruminating on this conversation for weeks afterward, I might forget it in a few minutes and move on to other, more pressing parenting or life matters.

That one piece of identity dramatically changes the whole valence of the moment and situation. It has implications for health and wellness, self-worth, my relationship with my children, not to mention my relationship with and the presence of my African American husband and his reaction and how that also influences the situation.

What Is Intersectionality?

Life is the intersection of the tangible and intangible, the mundane and extraordinary, pain and pleasure, light and dark. Life itself exists at the intersection. As such, we, as humans, are a manifestation of these intersections, which we call "intersectionality."

Intersectionality is when two or more things come together, ultimately making something unique from each thing as a singular entity because of their crossing or synergy. It exists on various planes—the way we think, our identity as a person, and our culture and communities.

To many conservatives, both Black and White, intersectionality can mean "because you're a minority, you get special standards, special treatment."

But when Columbia Law professor Kimberlé Crenshaw, who coined the term, was asked for a definition during a 2020 interview, she put it this way:

> These days, I start with what it's not, because there has been distortion. It's not identity politics on steroids. It is not a mechanism to turn White men into the new pariahs. It's basically a lens, a prism, for seeing the way in which various forms of inequality often operate together and exacerbate each other. We tend to talk about race inequality as separate from inequality based on gender, class, sexuality, or immigrant status. What's often missing is how some people are subject to all of these, and the experience is not just the sum of its parts.[1]

At its core, intersectionality recognizes that no one has a single identity. It acknowledges the importance of understanding how all our identities interact with each other. It also helps us recognize how people who inhabit multiple marginalized identities may be at an even greater disadvantage than those who only inhabit one or two.

For example, while it is true that most women in the US face discrimination based on their gender alone, WOC are especially vulnerable because they must contend with two forms of systematic oppression—sexism and racism—instead of just one. Felicia Davis Blakley, an interdisciplinary leader committed to intersectionality as a key to liberation, has experienced and continues to experience intersectionality in her personal and professional life beginning with what her mother told her:

> My mother and I had a conversation once where she said, "Listen. I'm fat, I'm Black and I'm a woman. That's all people see

when I walk through the door. That is it. You're Black and you're a woman. That's all people are going to see.

I was 10 or 11 and didn't really know what she was talking about. She was really explaining to me, before it was a word, intersectionality, that double jeopardy that you face. It's discriminatory.

In a lot of ways, she was right. People look at you and what they see is what they think you are. They don't see who you really are, or what's inside. I'm guilty of that too—not seeing the intersectionality of others, making assumptions.

The second part of that conversation was, "When you work, you need to do a good job. Your work needs to be impeccable. You need to do a good job for yourself and know that you've done that because it won't always be recognized."

That was profound. She's lived this life and she knew some of the realities that I was going to face. In the best way that she could, she was bracing me around that double jeopardy for that intersectional identity.

My mother also stressed to us the value of education. I think that was in part because we struggled a lot when I was a little girl with food insecurity, housing insecurity, and clothing insecurity.

She really connected that to her education and not having achieved her high school diploma and beyond. When I was 11, she went back to school. She had to take us with her because she didn't have a babysitter.

She received her GED at the local community college in our neighborhood. I can't tell you how profound that experience was to go to school with her, to see my mom as a human, a person trying to better herself. "If I tell you education is important, I have to show you, and to actually walk that walk." I saw her learn and be vulnerable to learning and get frustrated.

In her interview with *Time* magazine reporter Katy Steinmetz, Crenshaw explained that intersectionality is simply about how certain aspects of who you are will increase your access to the good things or your exposure to the bad things in life.[2]

Intersectionality in all its variations influences our choices, how people relate to us, how we relate to others, and how we think, act, and react. It also changes over time.

My intersectionality looked very different before having children. It looked different before getting a PhD. It looked different before moving to Arizona or Alabama or Chicago.

Like many other social-justice ideas, intersectionality stands because it resonates with people's lives, but because it resonates with people's lives, it's under attack. This can be seen in the current debates around critical race theory (CRT) in the US. CRT is an academic framework that examines how systemic racism intersects with other forms of oppression, such as classism and sexism, to shape people's experiences in society. Sadly, there's nothing new about defenders of the status quo criticizing those who are demanding that injustices be addressed.

A participant in one of our evaluations said, "White women don't have to see [intersectionality]; we die if we don't."

If we are not aware of intersectionality and the effect it has on our identity and day-to-day life, significant data on who we are, what influences us, and the depth of our experience goes unnoticed and untapped. Felicia deeply recognized this sentiment of the necessity of seeing through an intersectional lens in oppressive contexts. As she shares:

> But if you just look at healthcare and you look at maternal healthcare outcomes, in 2023 in the State of Illinois, a Black woman is six times more likely to die in childbirth or from childbirth complications.

The What and Why of Intersectionality

There have been famous stories around famous women—Beyoncé, for example—who have told their stories around not being listened to when they were in the hospital and risking some danger related to their pregnancies. The thing is, they are very wealthy women. You can say that those outcomes only happen for poor women, but the reality is that even when you norm for socioeconomic status and education, the disparity persists.

The risk of not addressing these intersectional things is that, in the healthcare context, women die. People die. Research has shown that what's at work is implicit bias. People are operating under a set of beliefs that they don't even know they have. It's just functioning in the background.

There are a lot of ways in which our symptoms or pains are discounted. Research has shown that the only way to really understand that is to accept that this is happening because of implicit bias among the providers.

In Illinois recently, there was a lot of required training for healthcare professionals around implicit bias. The goal is that if we start to talk about it and address it, we can decrease those outcomes.

In this one narrow instance, women and babies are dying. But you can take that same implicit bias around intersectional identities and you can apply it to all kinds of other things and have an understanding of the real peril that we're facing as a society because we haven't addressed this. If we don't address intersectionality, we're not fully addressing issues.

I almost died in childbirth with my third son. I remember feeling that something was wrong. I was pushing the help buttons, and I was dismissed by the first person. Then, a woman came in, and I was white as a ghost. She said, "Something is wrong." She sounded the alarm. I was hemorrhaging and bleeding out.

Everybody came in and they had to figure out where I was bleeding from and stop it. The woman who came in sat with me all night. She was a White nurse and somehow knew my family. They all worked for the county.

She said, "If anything happened to you, I could not explain to your uncle what happened." That woman sat in my room with me for the rest of the night. She knew that the first time that I called they dismissed me. If it happened again, maybe I would be too weak to call.

When I was in active labor, a doctor came in and she was giving me an exam. I said, "You are hurting me." She didn't alter what she was doing. I was in excruciating pain. I reached down there, and I grabbed her hand and pulled her hand out of me.

I said, "Stop! You are hurting me." At that point, my husband said, "Everybody get out. If you are not her doctor, get out. Put a sign on the door that the only person who is coming in this room is her doctor. She's not a guinea pig. She's in labor and in pain and this is high risk enough. It's stressful."

It's the fact that I said she was hurting me, but I had to grab her hand and pull it out of me to get her to stop. She said, "Somebody help. Somebody grab her." No, you stop. You stop hurting me. I had already had kids, so I have a high tolerance for pain.

The fact that I'm saying to this woman that whatever she is doing is not right and it is hurting me and then her reaction. She was apathetic and blamed me.

She didn't explain. She didn't even try. I am a live person. That disregard was callous. That is a mark of implicit bias, a huge and detrimental example of implicit bias.

Intersectionality and Leadership

With mental (or disciplinary) intersectionality, we see things more holistically. What do we see when science and art meet? Creative experimentation leading to innovations and new discoveries.

What do we see when psychology meets architecture? The creation of spaces that enhance life and influence how we relate to one another.

What do we get when mental and physical health meet? A well person. When we sit at the intersection of mental models and seemingly opposing ideas, we're able to construct a bigger, more vivid picture, and see more of the encompassing truth. With this sight, even more is possible around what we can do, create, or even be.

Cultural or identity intersectionality is the same. When one aspect of our cultural identity meets another, they change or color each other. There are many aspects and therefore infinite combinations, including ethnicity, age, profession, region, heritage, language, relationship status, parenthood, gender, sexual orientation, military status, type of municipality, and more.

Intersectionality contributes to the reality that there is more diversity within communities than between them. Take a sibling constellation: all children born of the same parents often show up in unique ways.

They may also be African American or Puerto Rican American or Japanese or Italian, in the same city and neighborhood, in the same house, in the same generation, but vary by birth order, gender, age, etc. These slight to significant variations influence their paths and personalities, how they're treated by their parents and others, as well as their outlook. As Felicia expounds:

I am a girl from the south side of Chicago in every sense of the word. I'm not only from the south side, I grew up on the far south side.

A lot of people are centered downtown, but where I lived—which was public housing—is so far south that most Chicagoans don't even realize that the city goes that far. I'm the oldest of four children to my mother, a single mom. She dropped out of high school when she became pregnant with me.

As a Black woman coming from the south side of Chicago, arguably the wrong side of the tracks, I had a lot of headwinds against me as far as what my outcome in life would be. I had people in the community and schools that said because my mom was a single mom and such and such, I was going to drop out of school. I probably wouldn't graduate high school. All of those lowered expectations were pushed on me.

In some respects, this Chicago enclave is pushed to the city limits and it's very secluded—not in an intentional, glamorous kind of way, but in a throw away, "these people have no value" kind of way.

The geography around the area is heavily industrial, contaminated, full of pollution and garbage dumps. There was a lot of what people today acknowledge as environmental racism. Then there was the isolation.

My mother grew up in Morgan Park. She was part of two really large families in the community that were well known. My grandfather married my grandmother, who both came from really large families.

We are all connected. "I am because you are." It's a notion of giving back. It wasn't philanthropy. Nobody was tossing around that fancy word when I was a kid. It was a responsibility that we have as a community.

The What and Why of Intersectionality

When I was in my early 20s, I started off with the Chicago Police Department in 1991. I grew up in the police department and in this organization.

I was at the police department for 10 years. The job afforded me the opportunity to see the city in a different way, not just my neighborhood or the neighborhoods that were adjacent to me.

It allowed me to go all over the city of Chicago and gave me a keen understanding of how the rest of the city looks, how the rest of the city is invested in different things, what resources are available to the rest of the city and then compare and contrast these things.

I understood there was a clear link between some of the problems we were having on the south and west sides that were clearly linked to economic opportunity, investment and community, school equality and all of those things. They were linked. As a police officer, you really do see it. It's not something people ask you about a lot, but you do see it.

For me, it drove the way in which I approached my job every single day and saw it as a responsibility. Most of the calls that you go to on a regular basis—until there is real system reform—are not 911 emergencies. They are situations where people don't know what to do. They just know the police will come.

Even if the question isn't a true police question, you can help them figure it out. "You need to go to this place. We can connect you to some counseling." It was a lot of life disorder issues, kids who won't go to school, rebellious teenagers, disputes between neighbors that aren't criminal.

I was a patrol officer for the first two years and then I became a youth officer, which meant I handled youth crime and referred a lot of kids to counseling and things like that. Then I also investigated the calls that came into the child abuse hotline.

Then I transitioned into being a violent crimes detective. I did that part of it for eight years. When I left, I was a violent crimes detective investigating sex-related offenses. A lot of the calls that came into the child abuse hotline were also sex-related offenses—not exclusively, but unfortunately the majority of them were.

When I was investigating the sex-related offenses, overwhelmingly the survivors were women and girls. You see the way in which our society doesn't really support the safety of women and girls as much as it should.

That was 10 years of my life. It's that experience that drives the view I take now in the work that I get to do.

Those outcomes don't have to be that way. With investment, with support, things can be different. My husband jokes that my answer for everything is wraparound services. With real investment and real infrastructure in our communities, we can address some of these things that are happening. We just haven't.

At the police department, though, it was the first time I felt the number one thing was me being a woman. Then it was my race. In that world, it's man, then woman. Then you start building the other distinctions. It's man/woman first for a lot of reasons.

Women weren't allowed in the police department for a long time. I had never experienced that except for in that context. But every other place, it's I'm Black and then the fact that I'm a woman.

That was 1991. At the time, I said I was going to be the first Black woman superintendent of police in Chicago. We still haven't had a woman or a woman of color.

In my intersectionality, I'm Black first. The police department was an anomaly. I am a Black woman. I came from a Black woman and I gave birth to a Black woman. It's important to me.

The What and Why of Intersectionality

In the course of history, Black women have had to know everybody's shit. Think about the amount of emotional intelligence required to know the needs and expectations of all of these people.

Black women were always triangulating. "What does this person want? What about this person?" It was about life or death. We had to know everybody else's issues, we had to be astute, and we had to respond to minute things that could mean our death—or severe harm if we didn't.

That is a wisdom that has been passed down from mothers to daughters for a long time. In the present-day context, think about the 2020 election. In that context, Black women saved democracy. Part of it is we have always had to show up in these big ways because we are still fighting for our own liberation. "Damn it. I have to pull you along kicking and screaming because I want to be free. I have to make you free too." Almost like Harriet Tubman.

I believe I'm a grower of people, community, and ideas. I've spent 12 years total in higher education administration. I see myself as a connector or facilitator where my mission is to educate and help people reach their full potential—to be a bridge. It's about investing in people with an eye towards creating change that's sustainable in our communities. A part of that is cultural intersectionality.

Through the lens of intersectionality, we are literally synergy. We are greater than any one part of who we are because of all the parts together. Me being an African American, second-generation Haitian mother of two children working in Chicago creates a cocktail of history, context, present, future, psychology, trauma, triumph, and possibility. Intersectionality is key to deepening our humanity and connecting us with others.

Within many of us, we experience both oppression and privilege. Oppression is the act or experience of being excluded from or a part of us or our expression being weakened or destroyed by an outside force.

Privilege is receiving something that we did not work for or earn that is not inherently a right. For example, if we were born with a trust fund or a house in our name, say given by our parents, we were born with that element of privilege. (Being given healthcare or free education would be considered a right and not a privilege.)

Some aspects of us are oppressed, starting before we were born, such as those based on skin color, gender, socioeconomic status, or sexual orientation. Others, like access to paid higher education, wealth, or property, are privileged aspects of our identity or experience.

Through each aspect, we can tap into a unified field or collective experience with others with that commonality. In this way, we can conceptually and logistically enhance our empathy and connection.

With more intention around our own intersectionality and what unites us and makes us unique, we can further develop our leadership and ability to unify and connect across seeming differences.

According to research studies around empathy, we have easier access to empathy and favoritism for those that look like us, whether it's in terms of appearance, race, ethnicity, or other characteristics. This phenomenon is often referred to as *in-group bias* or *homophily*. It means that people are more likely to feel a sense of connection and empathy toward others who are part of the same group or share similar characteristics.[3]

Thus, many WOC are in an opportune position to exercise empathic leadership for and in communities of color. In other words, WOC are also well-positioned in our intersectionality in uplifting our organizations and communities towards equity and liberation.[4]

While intersectionality is important in knowing ourselves, getting to know others, serving people, and supporting communities, we can't get stuck there. This is an important starting place but it's not the destination. The destination is love without the boundaries and associations of socially constructed identities.

When we get stuck on the color of skin, gender norms, labels of sexual preferences, or over-identifications of the social construct of age or generation, we lose sight of humans. I used to get stuck here. I used to fixate on someone being White or Black and what I thought that meant.

As part of a positionality statement, I wrote last year: in the spiritual realm, there is no skin color, material expression of gender, or division. There is only unity, only oneness, only love. I strive to live in this space and bring this underlying reality to our material experience.

Here, I remember that skin color and other points of difference are used as distractions from the truth and, worse, as excuses for oppression, greed, and power-mongering.

I too often get caught up in the forced and false reality of these divisions and the discussion of it, fighting for our humanity when we need to simply dwell in the truth. When we can tap into the spiritual reality of unity, we can manifest this experience in the physical realm.

I also recognize that I am in this body in this life, and this will shift, and my spirit may have another experience after this life. It's all an expression and experience of Spirit. In this way, we are all each other in this moment and beyond. We must balance the physical and spiritual realities. Felicia places this intangible aspiration into historical, sociopolitical, and practical relevance around intersectionality. As she shares:

The oldest women-focused organizations are right around 50 years old. It maps with women getting the ability to have a bank account. That's all part of second-wave feminism.

Overwhelmingly, second-wave feminism wasn't very intersectional. Just like with the suffrage movement, sometimes it's more expedient to leave your Black sisters behind than it is to say, "I will not vote until we all can vote." It's something that one could do but was not done. "Sure, let's push Black women aside and we, White women, will have the right to vote."

That's an important lesson for us in history. We shouldn't forget that. There cannot be another movement—especially in this gender space—where we pick off people and leave people behind.

One of the things I tell people about is Equal Pay Day. The day this is recognized shows how many days women have to work in a year to equal the amount of money that men made the year before. The further into the year, the less the women made compared to the men. But, every year marks the day that White women have not yet caught up to White men earning the same amount of money. A lot of people take that day and that figure —82 cents—to be what women are making. That's not what all women are making.

For working moms, that day is August 15. For Black women this year, that day was July 27. But for Hispanic women, that day comes in October. And for Native women, it comes in November. In November, at 54 cents. The goal isn't just to solve for the 82 cents—that's White women. Or to solve for the 63 cents for Black women. The goal is if we are inclusive in this movement, it's the 54 cents. We're trying to solve for the 54 cents. If we are doing anything less, we are leaving our sisters behind.

The What and Why of Intersectionality

Many second-wave feminist organizations didn't have that perspective fully. Racial identity wasn't as important as gender identity. There was a belief that "I'm a woman," but the only people that get looked at just as women are White women. There was a missed opportunity in understanding that the experiences of women of color are significantly different.

The goal is to make sure that we are including the experiences of all women, and we highlight those disparities and the inequities within the broader inequities in society. I want every woman and girl to see themselves reflected in our work, to see their intersectional identities reflected in our work.

In some respects, intersectionality has to be the air we breathe in order to achieve true liberation. I am not free while any woman is unfree, even when her shackles are different from my own. This liberation is a collective thing for Black women and women of color. It's 54 cents again. Our fates are tied to each other.

I've had my moments where it's hard to hold onto your center and your own intrinsic sense of self and value and worth. Especially if you're up against a world that doesn't see your worth, that doesn't hold those values for you. It's not easy, but we must dig into the reserves of resilience from all the women who came before. They changed things through their example. This is my leg of the relay race and I have to keep running my part and pass the baton to the next person.

I am working on leading in a way that I hope helps elevate others as I go along and helps them achieve their own liberation. I think about all the different aspects of ways in which I can help to make that change and move these levers.

I hope that there are a lot of other people who see their leadership that way—that the way they lead is creating pathways to liberation.

Chapter 8: The What and Why of Intersectionality

1. List the identities you hold and reflect on how they intersect in your life.
2. How do (or could) you express your full self in different environments?
3. What would it mean to embrace and share your whole self everywhere?

Felicia Davis Blakley

Felicia Davis Blakley (she/her) is a remarkable leader with a social conscience. A seasoned leader with a proven track record, Felicia has served in various positions in the government, public policy, higher education, and philanthropic sectors, gaining valuable experience and insights that few possess. Through her commitment to inclusive service to others, she has significantly impacted the community and inspired countless others to do the same.

As former president and CEO of the Chicago Foundation for Women (CFW), Felicia spearheaded strategic efforts to invest in cisgender women and girls and transgender and gender nonbinary individuals as catalysts for change. With an unwavering commitment, she fights for gender equity and building stronger communities for all. Her contributions and hard work have significantly influenced the foundation's vision and principles.

Preceding her notable role at CFW, Felicia worked in diverse executive positions in Chicago city government, including serving as inaugural executive director for the Mayor's Office of Public

Engagement, commissioner, and deputy mayor for public safety. Her diverse experiences have shaped her leadership style and direction, driving her to give back to the community and make a difference in the world.

Chapter 9
Cultural Self-Awareness

Culture is a mirror. It's a way to see a reflection of yourself and allows us to know our space and how we fit. We're not alone. We're part of many years and struggles of people. It's a way to fully see ourselves reflected.

— Xanat Sobrevilla

I was born a female, with brown skin, African, Haitian, French, and Dominican roots to a first-generation Haitian mother and an African American father from Mississippi, in Ann Arbor, Michigan.

At the age of two, my parents separated and from three on, I was also raised by a Polish-American, French Canadian dad.

I was mostly raised in a small, predominantly White rural town as one of four or five fellow youth of color in the town. Growing up, I had very different experiences depending on where I was and who I spoke to. I experienced blatant racism in some places and spaces but was also accepted and respected in others.

Cultural Self-Awareness

In my childhood and my past, the color of my skin was a point of trauma in my social experience, as I expressed in the introduction of this book.

I have my PhD in counseling psychology, and have lived in various parts of the US, including Alabama, Arizona, and now Chicago. For 10 years of my adult life (when I more intentionally shaped my identity, especially as a professional), I lived in Chicago on the south side, in a mixed-income, mixed-ethnicity, well-resourced neighborhood called Hyde Park.

I note this special neighborhood because I thought it embodied my culture, identity, and values in many ways: it was culturally and socioeconomically diverse, it had the feel of a walkable small town, and it was next to one of the largest lakes in the world.

However, this neighborhood and my experience up to this time is very different from the experience, look, and feel of many of the neighborhoods BECOME works with and in, also on the south (and west) side of Chicago.

It's the opposite in many ways: relatively high concentrations of financial struggle, lack of structural resources (restaurants, grocery stores with healthy whole foods), and disconnection from the apparent abundance of nature. While I have experienced being poor, I never felt poor.

For a while, we lived in a trailer park, but soon, my parents were able to buy an inexpensive house and worked hard on that house to make it what they dreamed.

I grew up religious but over the years have stepped into a more personalized exploration and connection to spirituality. My life colors how I see and experience the world and influences how I move through the work, as everyone's past and present experiences does. I've come to value love, family, community, relationships, history, growth, and commitment.

What about you? How do you live? What do you value? What are your traditions? Culture refers to all those things—the way a group or person lives, what they value, their spiritual or other daily practices, traditions, language, artifacts, and rituals.

Culture is a binding agent, uniting communities at different levels, be it ethnic, religious, regional, organizational, or otherwise. From a family to a nation, culture is ubiquitous. It is the glue that holds people together, and we can't escape its influence.

Culture not only holds our behaviors and values, motivations, and thought patterns in explicit and implicit ways—it shapes them. Whether through our cultural backgrounds or participation, values are often unconsciously influenced.

In some cases, cultural influence is loud and conspicuous, shaping who we are in ways that are undeniable. In other cases, its effects are quiet; its sources are ancient—it shapes us through familial practices and awareness, the teaching or passing along of traditions in daily, less structured ways.

Developing cultural self-awareness allows us to identify both the obvious and subtle cultural influences surrounding us and choose which ones we want to foster and which we want to let go or modify.

When we incorporate the integration of intersectionality into this journey of cultural awareness, we embark on a voyage of self-discovery. Each aspect of our identity illuminates novel worlds and uncharted territories. In failing to explore our own culture, we mindlessly adhere to implicit patterns instilled in us, which can often be detrimental to ourselves and others.

We live in three realms simultaneously: the body, the mind, and the spirit. My position exists in all of these, and my experience is shaped differently and convergently when seen through these lenses.

In my adult life, the color of my skin is a point of connection, advocacy, and empowerment. I'm now a mother of two young children. I'm a dreamer. I live in a world of imagination, visions, and possibilities. Sometimes I don't even see the limitation that is right in front of me because I'm too busy thinking of the possibility and pathway to getting there.

My consciousness has been shaped in large part by my family, including my extended family, and the religious and spiritual influences around me throughout my life. Education has also had a major influence, mostly my graduate education as a psychologist and researcher. I suspect that my PhD has opened doors that I'm not even aware of and may not have gotten through if I didn't have it.

Mentally, while I'm deeply entrenched in and love communities of color, I'm also very connected to the poor White and rural communities. They were my friends growing up, my first boyfriend, my neighbors, teachers, confidants, a source of heartache and pride.

At 10 years old, Brian was the first boy to ever ask me to be his girlfriend. I said yes. We walked home together. After a couple of days, he came knocking at my door, on Valentine's Day and broke up with me, saying that his mother wouldn't allow him to be with a Black girl.

A couple of years ago, I searched for him on Facebook. He was holding two guns and a blue lives matter sign, with car parts and a shed in the background. This was such an obvious example of how rearing influences your beliefs, values, and inclinations.

Since I often felt excluded in my life growing up, my research proclivities veer toward inclusive and constructivist ways of doing, learning, knowing, and changing. Due to frequent, direct experiences of injustice, my work has focused on justice.

However, lately, as a middle-aged, spiritually oriented woman, my mind is stepping beyond justice to transcendence and liberation, where we will all be free of this false reality and live fully in the highest truth of love, joy, and enlightenment.

My journey has been one so unlike Xanat's, yet in many ways, so much the same. As she shares:

> I was born in Mexico City, in De la Cruz, a few hours from the coast. My father's side is from Veracruz. My parents met in Mexico City, so I consider half of my family in Mexico City and half in Veracruz.
>
> My dad named me Xanat, which is a word in Tenek that means vanilla flower. They have a festival where they collect the vanilla flower. I take that as my dad wanting to keep that connection on that side. Other than that, I still haven't been able to go deeper.
>
> I came to the US when I was nine as part of an economic migration two years after NAFTA [North American Free Trade Agreement]. My dad's side had family in Chicago, so the thinking was that we could come to the US and try to stabilize.
>
> I came to Chicago in '96 and have been undocumented since. Through a program called DACA [Deferred Action for Childhood Arrivals], I am able to have a work permit. My parents were lower middle class in Mexico, struggling. When NAFTA came into being in '94, there was a big economic impact on Mexico. As I'm seeing it and talking with other folks that experienced it, it came with waves that impacted the time you were hit.
>
> My parents had connections with people in the US—my dad's family—and saw migration as a lifeline of sorts and a temporary solution. We left a very closeknit network of family on my mom's side to come and live with family on my dad's side in the hope that somehow we could have some sort of financial stability.

Cultural Self-Awareness

Prior to us migrating, I remember there were a lot of arguments and fighting, the stress that comes with poverty. My dad didn't have a stable job and my parents felt the stress of providing for me and my sister when the economic situation in Mexico was deteriorating. NAFTA was hitting Mexico disproportionately and there was a sense of increased stability in the US.

There are a lot of reasons for migration. To me, it was mostly economic or at least that was the root of it. Then, there's the typical story that we tell ourselves as immigrants—that our parents came here to give us a better life.

I don't know how much I buy into that whole bootstrap story, but my parents thought it would be more stable for my sister and me. College was thought of as how you obtain stability. Or we could find a way for my sister and me to adjust even if they had to exist as undocumented themselves.

I came with both parents and my younger sister. In 2011, I graduated from college and started to hear about organizers in Chicago who were undocumented and came together because there was a person in removal proceedings in 2009. I started going to their meetings and getting to know them. That's how I came into organizing.

I was aware. I knew what my status was and I knew the challenges pretty quickly. For some people, it comes after learning a little bit about what it means to be undocumented or why. I became part of the culture of the undocumented and it shaped me.

Our parents made the best choice that they could at that moment. It was a difficult choice. It felt like home in that we were already recognizing our circumstances.

We had to figure out what's after higher education when you have no papers, or access to what's next. Work? Being able to be here, I learned that there are a lot of folks who would have to deal with the criminal/legal system and were in removal proceedings.

In 2013, I decided to focus on supporting people in removal proceedings and that's how we came to form OCAD [Organized Communities Against Deportations]. I'm one of the co-founders.

In founding the organization, there were a lot of conversations around where we stand as privileged within the undocumented community. I went to college. I speak English. I knew how to navigate or have some connections/resources to navigate.

IYJL, which is what we were before—Immigrant Youth Justice League—we centered our experiences, we formed what we wanted to advocate and push for locally and nationally.

Since then, we have had a lot of conversations around the privileges we have. After 2012 some of us obtained DACA, and that allowed us to have work permits, and we're now considered "not a priority" for removal. For some of us, that offered some protection when it came to being public about our status.

In 2013, many of us decided to continue organizing and utilize the knowledge and skills we had acquired. At that point, we decided to continue to grow our networks and build with people still considered priorities for removal. We decided to focus solely on anti-deportation campaigns. By 2020, I became a full-time organizer with OCAD.

Organizing has been my method for survival and the thing that gives me hope and energy. It's the means to change the conditions and the ability for me or others to then be able to thrive. It is what, right now, allows me to find my people and exist in this moment.

Xanat's story reflects the many layers and facets of culture and its sources. Culture comes out of nations, from cities, through villages and tribes, passed on from family to family, and sprouts from political decisions and macro-level movements. While it shapes us, it can also push us, force us, and smother us.

Xanat's cultural background led her to be both a humble and triumphant leader. She didn't see her leadership capabilities for a long time and fell into active leadership for survival. Now, her leadership uplifts her as well as hundreds of others. Her cultural awareness is keen, and she shows just how powerful, binding, and uplifting culture can be:

> Everything I've learned, or do, or that is important to me goes back to culture. It is the traditions and beliefs that we hold as people no matter where we are—Mexico City or Chicago.
>
> It's something that creates a certain form of identity. Immigrants are not just one culture, even in the Mexican community. I'm from Mexico, and when I started to know other undocumented folks, many were also from Mexico and others were from South Korea and Palestine.
>
> As a group of young undocumented people, we started to note the things that made it difficult for us to thrive and understand the varying risks implied by our organizing. Culture is an interesting thing to navigate within immigrants.
>
> Because of our focus on immigration, we have a unique perspective on culture as we strive to organize with people from different cultures. People who have been affected by US culture and other people who have not been so affected by US culture because they're just coming here. They have yet to be indoctrinated by US culture.
>
> Language, artifacts, the tools we use, what we value, some of our stories and rituals—they're shared among the group.
>
> Recently, I have been wanting to learn more about my dad's side. As a child immigrant who came and had to learn English and see

the differences in US culture and my culture, I adhered to that identity as a way to not assimilate or lose myself. As an immigrant, one is confronted by assimilation as a survival mechanism.

As a kid, I always wanted to go back. My family in Mexico City is warmer and more of a network of support. That's what I remembered. When I got permission to leave the country for a month, I thought of what a difference it would have been to grow up with my cousins and my aunts. I have a large family there. That experience shifted how I experience life.

Often when you feel uprooted from your support networks you want to go back your values of connectedness and support: the food, the warmth, and the skepticism of politics. When you're in a country that experienced a lot of instability, you tend to become more skeptical of politics and the judicial system.

I don't want to assimilate or lose myself or my culture. Also, recognizing that some of the struggles that I have experienced here as a brown Latina person rise from rejection. I want to connect to my roots and not lose those things.

Embracing our culture and not fully assimilating or seeking ways to keep our culture is our way of saying no to the conditions that have created our displacement or have allowed for us to be seen as not worthy. It's finding pride in our lineage and backgrounds to confront what we are facing.

It's a way to take home with you wherever you are. I found other people who were undocumented and migrated around the same age and had similar experiences as a child. When you have people that you can share rituals or knowledge with, then you create a home even though we're not in Mexico.

Preserving our culture as immigrants can enable us to establish a sense of home in unfamiliar territory. Many yearn for the comfort of familiar foods, and while some ingredients may not be readily available, we find ways to recreate them. Ultimately, we endeavor to cultivate a feeling of home wherever life takes us.

The way we celebrate together has tremendous significance. Whether we're protesting outside ICE [Immigration and Customs Enforcement] offices, or engaging with music, chants, and food, it instills in us an immense sense of pride and strength.

Our unique rituals may not always resonate with everyone present, but they bind us together and distinguish us from what we're fighting against. Pride is incredibly powerful, and it allows us to forge connections and experience happiness with one another.

As an immigrant, sometimes your immediate family is so much smaller because the rest of your family is in your home country. It's a nice way to still try to experience those things with a group of people.

Cultures can also clash, like oil and water. One culture can influence another—quiet, reshape, squash, or quell. Given our intersectionality, we're influenced by different cultures. The deleterious and strengthening effects of different cultures show through Xanat's story clearly. Some cultures, like the US culture, oppress, divide, fragment, and skew our thinking, even distract us from the most important things in life, like relationships and self-awareness.

Xanat had to be wise to the culture she was in (the US) and strive to hold onto the culture she valued, her root culture. To do this, she had to know both and keep both in her conscious awareness. What rang loudly and exquisitely to me was the profound effect of celebration. They celebrated their culture, which gave them energy and fuel to persist.

While the various elements of culture are so clear in Xanat's story, culture is often murky in many of our stories. It takes digging, inquiry, reflection, seeking, and connection to unearth the varied cultural tapestry that makes us *us*. However, regardless of the work, the energy is well worth the discovery and the ultimate effect it can have on us, our communities, and those we serve.

Chapter 9: Cultural Self-Awareness

1. What have you learned about yourself or your community that inspires hope and strength?
2. Which moments of learning have shaped you, and who contributed to them?

Xanat Sobrevilla

Xanat Sobrevilla (she/her), an accomplished activist, is a highly respected figure in the fight against deportation. As the leading force behind the Organized Communities Against Deportations (OCAD) campaign and coalition efforts, she works tirelessly to support anti-deportation campaigns and ensures that OCAD plays a significant role in the Erase the Gang Database Coalition.

Xanat's advocacy efforts have extended to pushing back against government surveillance tactics that unfairly target immigrants for deportation. Her work is grounded in a dedication to the cause of collective liberation and her commitment to the fight for social justice.

Before her current role with OCAD, Xanat was actively engaged with the Immigrant Youth Justice League. There, she honed her passion for advocating on behalf of immigrant communities. Her extensive experience and fierce determination make her a leading voice in the fight for immigrant rights.

Xanat's tireless efforts toward the cause of social justice have helped create positive change and improve the lives of countless people.

Chapter 10
Intersectional Practices for Organizations

My entire life has been incredibly intersectional. As a woman of color, being, learning, having a learning difference, just not fitting in the standard society, I've had to think about things in intersectional ways.

Being Black in a society that didn't value my melanin, I remember hearing several times as a little girl (it was supposed to be a compliment but it was very much a negative), people would say, "You look so cute for a dark-skinned girl."

Dealing with the intersectionality of having a learning difference, I wasn't educated on my learning difference. I had to educate myself in undergraduate school and in graduate school about my differences. I wasn't taught to treat my neuroatypical learning style as a strength. My mother taught me it was a strength, but at school, it was definitely not viewed as a strength.

I was raised in a suburb of Chicago, and I had a very active and energetic family, but my parents were separated throughout most of my childhood.

Early in my life, I was forced to think about what it meant to be a young Black girl whose mother's family spoke Spanish and celebrated Puerto Rican identity.

— Keisha Farmer-Smith

Given that the whole person is a cultural entity, as well as a spiritual, emotional, social, and experiential being, a healing space needs to both emulate and welcome this wholeness. Our apparent identities only provide a glimpse into what we *may* be experiencing in the world. These visible, and even invisible identities are gateways to our story, as with Keisha's learning difference. They are entry points to the many layers of our humanity and life experience.

In creating spaces, be it organizations, blocks, or social clubs, that welcome and respond to the whole person, we can make ways for openness and storytelling. We can create internal cultures of connection.

These spaces need to value culture, complexity, self-exploration, and cultural navigation altogether. Cultural navigation is the ability to navigate and engage effectively within different cultural contexts. It involves understanding, respecting, and adapting to cultural norms, values, beliefs, and practices when interacting with people from diverse backgrounds.

Cultural navigation is the journey we take in exploring our cultural identities and the communities that influence us. When we question and open ourselves to this journey in the work, purpose, or living space, we can step more intentionally into our more aware and higher selves and connect authentically with each other.

This concept and practice of cultural navigation is particularly relevant in diverse and multicultural societies or when engaging in cross-cultural interactions. It is just as important in personal and professional settings as it is in community settings.

It promotes mutual understanding, respect, and collaboration across cultures, and ultimately fosters inclusivity and reduces misunderstandings or conflicts that may arise from cultural differences.

And, we must remember that there is more diversity within a group than between groups. Our intersectionality points to the complexity of being human. Both Keisha and I are Black women, born of immigrants, in families that spoke a language in addition to English growing up, in proximal generations, and mothers of two kids.

Amid our many commonalities, there are vast and important differences in our experience and the way we see the world. My Haitian background and Keisha's Puerto Rican background add texture to some of this difference. The places of our rearing, our focus areas in education, and our sibling constellations add complementarity in our collective diversity.

At BECOME, we've had conversations about positionality (our identity in relation to the work), and we talk about the multifaceted nature of culture. This includes exploring our own cultural intersectionality, stereotypes we hold about others or our own, and assumptions about communities and the work.

When we connect with our own experience in context and then listen and absorb another's, we can walk together in sync. Intersectionality is an opportunity for us to step into each other even more.

Here are a few characteristics of organizations or spaces that welcome present and changing intersectionality:

- Being flexible and nimble to respond to and address changing professional and personal needs and goals
- Prioritizing learning about the whole person, not just professional competencies and skills

Intersectional Practices for Organizations

- Encouraging and making space and time for people to reflect and explore their positionality and intersectional identities both independently and collectively

We also have to remember that intersectionality changes over time. For example, as I grew older, had children, grew in my career, my priorities changed, and so did the communities I considered myself a part of. Keisha also recognized the shifting identities over time and how this builds our intersectionality. As she offers:

I first discovered intersectionality in high school when a wonderful literary expert exposed me to the work of bell hooks. And I started reading the poetry and the short stories of Dr. hooks and them talking about the difficulty navigating white, heteronormative Christian society as a black queer woman. And at the same time, they write about the importance of being able to decipher and understand the rules of white, heterosexual men.

The normativity of that society, that is, the paradigm that we live under affects how we're reared. I was born in the '70s, and my mama told me that when I was born, she couldn't even get a credit card. Wow. Women couldn't get credit cards in the '70s. It wasn't until the late '70s that her husband, who she was separated from, had to sign a letter saying that she could have a credit card. So I was raised under that gaze of machismo. That was the societal machismo that I, and other girls like me, born in the '70s, faced.

There are also some epistemological intersectional privileges that I have now. For example, I'm highly educated. That's a privilege. I was raised as a Christian, and that's an intersectional privilege. At the same time, I was also raised dealing with, living with, and having to face some intersectional challenges.

Here are a few skills of leaders who embrace their intersectionality as well as others:

- **Self-awareness.** Being able to see one's thoughts, feel one's feelings, and name one's internal conditions and dynamics, including reactions and possibilities.
- **Self-reflection.** This skill includes being able to look at oneself nonjudgmentally and allow one to see all aspects of oneself.
- **Reflexivity.** This is similar to self-reflection but takes a critical lens in looking at one's work or actions and how we can respond and improve.
- **Unconditional positive regard** for self and others.
- **Humanizing.** Being able to see past color and cultural identity (ironically) to see the person as human, as a soul experiencing this life through this body at this time.

BECOME's work is about community-driven transformation. It's about people knowing and stepping into their potential and welcoming others around them to do the same. A large part of BECOME's work helps people and organizations, especially in or serving historically oppressed communities, to navigate effective and lasting positive change towards an ideal.

Keisha's leadership and perspective at BECOME are beautifully layered and center on story and responsiveness. Story in the context of life, community, and society invites us into a deeper understanding of each other. When we can understand each other better, we can grow together.

We use evaluation as a tool for transformation. It's a process of knowing and amplifying the impact of a program, policy, or initiative. Keisha speaks about how intersectionality guides her in evaluation work but also shapes the change we are making and want to see:

Intersectional Practices for Organizations

I find my strength and my power in intersectionality. There is strength and power in being culturally humble and culturally respectful, having an open mind, and being willing to learn from other people. I don't care what ethnicity or culture or lifestyle orientation they are; they/we are all humans. And so that is how I approach my work and my evaluation analysis. I am unapologetically intersectional in my analysis.

Even when I look at qualitative data [words, stories, experiences], I filter the data by age, by gender, by ethnicity. I want to hear the story of what's being told to me.

It is essential to be inclusive and participatory, first to take a step back and learn about the humanity of the person whose data I'm looking at.

So, for example, right now, we [BECOME] are working with a community-based group in Chicago that assists community members in accessing and buying housing. Now, to respect and understand people's story, it's not just good enough for me to say, "oh, okay, well, these are all the Puerto Ricans, and the Puerto Ricans are saying this." Or "these are all the Black seniors, and they're saying this."

It's important to not just hear their stories, but to respect their unique experiences and to work with them to explore what equity looks like given their intersectional background. What does safety look like? What does community safety look like for you as a Polish-speaking, middle-aged woman or as a Puerto Rican mother of three little boys? What does your humanity look like? And how does that inform the work that we need to do?

It's when communities listen to the needs of residents and when we, as researchers, listen to the stories and the experiences and treat those people as content experts of their own experience, that that we get to the root of things.

I feel it helps me to act as an ally. I feel that it helps me to work with them when we're doing strategic planning for their organizations or within their community space. Understanding people's experiences and the story of their lives—it helps us get to not just solutions but culturally responsive and inclusive, and equitable solutions. It helps us to meet people where they are.

That is when we can begin to usher in sustainable change.

Just as we want to make change in the outside world, we must first look and work inward—in ourselves, in our relationships, in our organizations, and in our own communities.

What are my values—my underlying, motivating values? What drives my decisions and behavior? What do my teammates or neighbors value? What is the story that led to those values? These types of questions can unlock family history, cultural mores, hopes and dreams, and even pain points. Understanding people's stories based on their culture and the intersectionality of their lives helps us to help each other and others better. As Keisha expounds:

I didn't grow up with violence, but I grew up with the concept of machismo. It's the idea that you fix your brother's plate. You fix your father's plate. You girls do this, girls stay in the house, girls do laundry. I was raised with those concepts, and I was also raised by a woman who was very womanist and pushed back against that shit. My mother is the first doctorate in our family. She earned her EdD. I'm sitting here looking at her diploma. She set the tone for every single woman in my family.

Our collective intersectionality can constitute the social fabric that can serve as a foundation and a safety net when woven intentionally. When we attend to our stories, see the humanity in each other, and respond across time, everyone elevates. As Keisha adds:

We try our best to do that at BECOME as much as possible. Telling and hearing our stories can help you get to some of the difficult questions that need to be asked to see the humanity in someone. It helps us talk about really difficult issues. Do you feel included or excluded? Do you feel a part of this community? Why or why not? Do you feel safe at your school or workplace? Why or why not? And so if you're really going to get to that depth of knowledge, you have to be intentional about talking and learning about people's intersectionalities.

Chapter 10: Intersectional Practices for Organizations

1. What did you learn by deeply listening to someone's story?
2. How can organizations create spaces that honor and respond to people's lived experiences?

Keisha Farmer-Smith

Dr. Keisha Farmer-Smith (she/they) has partnered with Chicago-area organizations dedicated to supporting safe, healthy spaces for youth for 25 years. Her past youth development experience includes supervising program outcomes and impact at Boys and Girls Clubs of Chicago; serving as director of programs at Family Focus Inc.; managing gender-specific after-school programs at Alternatives, Inc.; and coordinating educational and vocational services for the Illinois Department of Children and Family Services youth at Uhlich Children's Advantage Network.

An experienced evaluation specialist, Keisha was an integral part of both Chicago Community Trust's LGBT Community Needs Assessments and served as the evaluation designer and methodological lead for Morten Group, reporting on data collected from over 2,000 respondents. Her work supports evaluation tool design, participatory data collection efforts, and outcomes analysis

with an emphasis on strengths-based and participatory models.

Keisha is a professionally trained social worker, with graduate degrees in counseling and urban planning. She earned a PhD in public policy analysis from the University of Illinois with research that applied participatory action to evaluate outcomes for youth development programs. She is a 2010 Berkowitz Award winner for Outstanding Service to Children and a founding board member of the Chicago Freedom School. A longtime resident of the Pullman and Cottage Grove Heights community areas, Keisha enjoys gardening, volunteers with her block club, is a member of Delta Sigma Theta Sorority Inc., and is a proud mother of two adult sons.

Her leadership at BECOME has led organizational partners to greater clarity, deeper connection with communities, and amplified impact.

Section Four

Power: Activating and Using our Power Responsibly

Using power responsibly—as a means, not an end—refers to employing power or influence in a purposeful and ethical manner to achieve specific goals or outcomes, rather than seeking power solely for personal gain or domination. It emphasizes using power as a tool or resource to serve a greater purpose, rather than viewing power as an ultimate objective in itself.

When we use our power as a means, we can harness it to address societal challenges, create opportunities, and affect positive change. When we use our power responsibly, we focus on leveraging it to advance a cause, promote justice, facilitate collaboration, or support the empowerment of others, rather than solely pursuing personal ambition or dominating others.

Chapter 11
Using Power for Good

My dad called me baby girl. He was sitting there beside me in Dr. Jones's office for a scheduled meeting to "discuss my future." Dr. Jones, the guidance counselor, told him that I probably wasn't capable of much—that essentially I didn't have much academic potential.

The school had given me some tests—three or four tests I barely remembered being pulled out of class for.

Dr. Jones explained to me and my dad that these tests showed that I was, most likely, dyslexic. At the time, they also said I had attention issues. There was no full diagnosis—just a few tests.

It's not that I was a discipline problem. I didn't get in trouble. I wasn't disruptive in class. I had attention issues. After testing me and looking at my results, Dr. Jones said he really felt I would be happier and more comfortable in vocational education classes.

He told my dad that there were plenty of jobs for "people like me," and asked me if I wanted to become a hairstylist.

My father listened patiently to Dr. Jones, then turned to me and said, "Baby girl, you wanna be a beautician? There's nothing wrong with that." And I said, "No, I don't wanna be a beautician."

And he said, "well, what do you wanna be?" And I said, "I think I wanna be a lawyer or a politician." My dad looked right at that man, and he said, "Don't move my daughter. Don't touch her. Don't change a single class. You do not have my permission to move her out of her classes."

Then, my dad said, "She said she wants to be a lawyer or a politician, and that's what she wants to be. And, if she's trying as hard as she can, that's okay with me." Wow. Then, he patted my hand and grabbed it, and we walked out of that counselor's office. That's power in action—to know what you want and to take action to get it.

— Keisha Farmer-Smith

With so many people or organizations determined to "use their power for good," the question is, what does that mean exactly? We all agree that using power for good is essential if we want to create positive change, promote equity, and create a more just and compassionate society. But what does power in action look like? Keisha experienced power in action firsthand as a teenager.

Using one's power responsibly means to influence and make a helpful difference in your own life and the lives of others. It means having a positive impact on people, communities, and broader society. It means using power intentionally and with accountability. This includes being accountable for the consequences of one's actions. It means actively working to ensure that power is wielded in a manner that respects the rights and well-being of others.

You don't have to have a title, a big office, a lot of money, or a team of enforcers to use your power for good. You just need to be a champion for yourself and others. Power, among other things, means supporting and encouraging others through their journey, whether through life, education, employment, or self-exploration. As Keisha conveys:

> My parents have been champions for my education. They have been incredibly supportive all through my schooling. When I got my dual master's degrees, I went back to my high school.

> Mr. Jones was retiring but I made sure to make it known that the little girl he wanted to send to beauty school had gotten a double master's degree in urban planning and in community counseling. Later, when I got my doctorate, I didn't have to go back to let them know. The school reached out to me.

> And so, anytime I feel stuck, or I feel challenged, I really try to channel that kind of power—the power to speak up, to stand up for myself or someone else. I remember the love that my parents had and the dedication they showed to me. The most powerful thing they taught me was that quitting is not an option.

What is Power?

Do you know how powerful you are?

We define *power* in this book as *personal power,* or the ability to work or influence self, people, and events. We believe power is both mental and spiritual in nature, and often latent or under-used. We believe the power in most of us is waiting to be activated to its full potential, often through our ability to balance our masculine and feminine energies.

We believe personal power comes from a person's attitudes, and state of mind rather than the formal power of authority such as rank, titles, degrees, status, or appointments. It comes from an awareness of, and owning, our culture as WOC, and as survivors, creators, and "thrivers."

Power is a complex and multifaceted concept. When we oversimplify it, or have a limited understanding of its dynamics, we do ourselves and our own power a disservice.

Power is often equated with the idea that it is strictly about physical strength or force (masculine energy). However, it's more textured. Power can manifest and be used on all levels, in various forms, including social, political, economic, or intellectual power.

Another misconception is that power is inherently evil or corrupt. WOC and other oppressed groups in society too often believe power is negative or dangerous and therefore pass up opportunities. While power *can* be used to exploit or oppress others, it is not inherently negative or dangerous. While it *can* be misused and lead to corruption, it is not an absolute rule. Many people who have tapped into their power use their influence to bring about positive change. It's important to note, though, that others, often through no conscious intent, have a negative impact without realizing how powerful even a word can be.

Some people mistakenly believe that power is a finite resource— for one person or group to gain power, another must lose it. However, power can be generated, shared, expanded, and infinite. It's like oxygen in the air we breathe—there's enough to go around.

Like Keisha, Jenise Terrell has experienced the nuanced nature of power:

> We were a very matriarchal family. I come from a family where there were far more women leading households. My great-grandmother was the head of our family. We were sharecroppers in Kentucky. She helped lead her family north in the 1950s, where they could secure factory jobs. They bought property and lived middle-class lives while maintaining a strong tie to our Kentucky roots, to all the branches of the family, to the church. That was my Nana.

She was a very traditional woman. She would tell me, "Your mom did a great job raising you girls. I'm so proud of you. The only thing I wish is that you went to church a little bit more." She had a wry sense of humor and a keen way of serving a lesson while also giving you praise.

Because of her, my definition and understanding of power was nuanced. I understood from her the power of choosing your words wisely. You can build someone up or break them down, depending on how you frame your message. Institutions, like people, have similar choices in the exercise of power.

One formal definition of power is the ability to perform, do something, or take a particular action. This definition reflects an internal drive, internal capacity. The other is the capacity or ability to direct or influence the behavior of others or the course of events. That's external.

When I talk about this relationship between my great-grandmother and others, there is a power there.

My uncle is another great example. He stands firm in who he is as a man amid a lot of powerful women, loving, welcoming, and facilitative of our family. That's power. It's shared power. This is what I bring to the table. I also honor what you bring to the table. That, too, can be power.

As I've matured, I've come to understand that power is neither inherently good nor bad. Power is defined by how it is wielded. The ability to influence, create, and to move things forward doesn't always have to be negative.

I believe power comes from inside us. My former boss and mentor Sherman Hill embodied protective power. If I were to select an avatar for Sherman, it would be a pit bull. He built a career working in the juvenile justice system during the 1960s, fighting for our young people.

To protect young black children in the juvenile justice system, Sherman had to learn to use the rules and regulations to the advantage of the young people he served. Throughout his career he continued to use his knowledge of regulations to fight systems and ensure access to information and resources for those he served.

I learned from Sherman the value of being well-steeped in your trade. Know the rules better than your competitors, better than those with positional authority, so you can use them to get what you need. Effective power lies in understanding the gulf between how things are supposed to work and how they actually work.

If you think about each of the women in this book, you can see how the power dynamics of their lives and circumstances changed over time. Just because a person, group, organization, or political group influences things on a macro level today doesn't mean they'll be able to have the same level of influence tomorrow, or next week, or next year.

Societal shifts, age, changes in leadership, culture, laws, political changes, and evolving circumstances can alter power structures quickly. Power shifts can lead to shifts in influence and authority, and culture. Be patient.

Power can be fluid and extend beyond formal positions or titles—like the power children have in our lives to shift our perspective or direction, or the power of mothers and grandmothers. As Jenise offers:

> Motherhood is power. Certainly, what I experienced with my mother and what I tried to shape with my children took power. I had a very clear sense of where I came from, our history not only as a family—knowing that we were from Kentucky, knowing that we were sharecroppers.

Using Power for Good

From the time that I was little, I was given familial history and knew that we could trace our roots back to George Dickerson, who is my great-grandmother's grandfather. We couldn't go further because he was an enslaved man who changed his name. We don't know what his former name was, but we know George Dickerson started this beautiful family. Calling the names of our ancestors, recalling their legacy is caretaking of the past. This caretaking preserves the roots that allow the tree to grow. That's power.

I felt empowered by the knowledge of our family's history and the sacrifices made by each generation to propel us forward. Similarly, my mother ensured that my sister and I were steeped in Black history.

After I went through eighth grade at the all-Black Catholic school, I went to a suburban 95% White school. Talk about culture shock. Night and day. I remember thinking, when I encountered folks who tried to deter me from taking advanced courses, "These people clearly don't know who I am."

That is the gift of power, of knowing where you come from. I knew my stuff. I am the daughter of Ann, who is the daughter of Patricia, who is the daughter of Mamie Lee. I carry all of them with me.

Know who you are so that you can stand in the present and be clear about what's ahead.

Another misconception is that power is all about dominance. True power is not about control or dominance of others. Power can involve influencing, directing, or uplifting others, fostering collaboration, and creating an environment where everyone's potential is maximized.

Power's Shadow

However, there are people that use their power in destructive ways. As inspirational and motivating as stories about positive power can be, it is beneficial to realize that not everyone will, or does, see positive power as powerful, or for the greater good. Even a positive truth can be deemed a negative power, Jenise shares:

> Early on, I was aware of the negative influence external agents had on my life and my community. I experienced power in this context as harmful, coercive, someone's ability to exert authority that is not aligned with the very people impacted.
>
> I rebelled against traditional, formal power exercised in this way. What I didn't understand and what I didn't see initially, is that power can be exercised differently.
>
> In 2015, I took part in an organizational strategic planning session. The facilitator launched the session with general questions inviting us to speak candidly about the organization and its future direction.
>
> I was a junior staffer and I felt empowered by the question. I stepped into the opportunity, "I'm just going to say it. This is who we are, this is what we stand for. This is what success looks like and this is what differentiates us from everything else." I remember walking away and feeling good about speaking in earnest.
>
> After the meeting, I received detracting feedback from a leader in the organization—someone who wielded power through intimidation.
>
> I didn't realize it at the time, but this person was threatened by my voice, by my leadership, so they had been trying to diminish my influence in the organization.

In that moment, when I took the liberty to freely contribute my observations and vision, I was seen. It didn't matter what my detractor said. I didn't even care. I didn't care about what happened after that. I had said my piece.

When you step into a space and completely give yourself over to what you believe and what you think, it's noticeable. It impacts the room. It shifts the energy.

I walked away satisfied, not because of what I expected to happen, but because I was standing fully and powerfully in my truth and gave my greatest contribution to the organization in that moment. As a result of that, I was seen and ultimately afforded new opportunities to lead within the organization.

The leader Jenise mentioned used their power to try to have dominance over and quell her voice, but she didn't allow that. She used her power to motivate herself through the challenge and still stood in her truth and expression.

Power can have a shadow, even positive power, especially when we exercise power in isolation or hierarchy. Just because we have power or power is ascribed to us through our title or position doesn't mean we feel powerful. If you're in a formal "position of power," you often have significant responsibilities—some of which you didn't have a voice in having.

You may be the person who makes the important decisions that impact others, but you wonder if you have the knowledge or leadership skills to make those decisions—especially at first. As a leader, the ultimate responsibility of the position and your power rests on your shoulders. You may not always have someone to rely on for guidance or support.

While BECOME strives for collective leadership and egalitarian organizational structures, hierarchy is the dominant way of doing things in most organizations historically and currently. The higher you go, the fewer people there may be with whom you can share your concerns or discuss sensitive matters. The higher up in any organization you're in, the harder it is to find people who truly understand the challenges and pressures that come with the position.

The weight of decision making, the need to meet the expectations of your organization and team, and the constant scrutiny from others can be overwhelming. Walking alone in power means carrying a lot of burdens largely on your own. The stress can take a toll on your mental and emotional well-being. Finding trusted advisors and establishing trustworthy relationships is critical for success. Jenise expounds:

> Positional leadership can be lonely if you presume that it has to be done by yourself. The people that are holding me up right now as a new CEO, helping feed my sense of possibility and wonderment about what is possible, are the women I work with on my leadership team.
>
> It's the women, advisors, and coaches I have in my corner. It is the women who say nothing but, "I see you. Congratulations. I'm so proud of you. I'm so happy for you." They keep me afloat.
>
> It's my grandmother and my great-grandmothers who empower me—and they're not even in this realm, but I feel it.

Jenise's start as the CEO of Public Allies gave her the direct experience of both the light and shadow of what many call "positional power"—authority ascribed to others due to a title or position. Whether it's power's light or shadow we experience at any moment, we, and others, benefit from self-awareness and intentionality. We have experienced the fact that people with strong personal power are self-aware. They are focused on their self-efficacy. They hone their ability to empathize, cooperate, and communicate with others—especially if they are operating from awareness and centeredness in their feminine power.

Feminine Power

To birth a new structure, systems, and collective practices, we must tap into a balance of masculine and feminine energy, a balance of doing and creating, listening, and supporting. We must move beyond our current modus operandi of Western culture and focus on the possibilities of the future yet rooted in presence and being.

The creative energy we've lost for so long is the feminine principle. Many people of all genders have shunned the feminine, be it consciously or subconsciously, believing the lies that it is "weak" and ineffective. For too long we've failed to see why it's needed, how it's needed, or the power in it.

The masculine principle has been predominant in the US since our origin as a sovereign nation. It is not the masculine energy that has caused our current chaos, but a profound imbalance and emphasis and reliance on the masculine that has contributed to, if not caused, the current calamity.

Regardless of our biological sex, whether we are cis-gendered or transgendered women or nonbinary people, we all have a mix of masculine and feminine energy. The feminine and masculine energies we're referring to are in all living beings, and even in many inanimate, electric things. Both are required for the creation and perpetuation of all forms of life. However we identify, we need both kinds of energy in our daily lives, in our personal and professional lives, and in how we choose to lead others.

The feminine rises and becomes resilient in the face of ongoing trauma and subjugation. These additional qualities cultivate the type of femininity that is needed now, more regularly showing up in women of color due to our cultural mores and collective, historical experience.

Fellow WOC, this is a call to you, first and foremost, to recognize, welcome, and manifest your latent and overt leadership power. Ever since women began seeking leadership in a male-dominated world, they believed they had to mimic or emulate the male style of leadership because that's all most of us, men and women, knew.

Most of us have learned or been taught to respect the more masculine or traditional leadership style—adopting it over the scientifically proven feminine style, one of empathy, collaboration, communication, and emotional intelligence.

Historically, leadership positions have been dominated by men, which has led to the perception that a male-energetic style of leadership is more effective or appropriate. People of all genders and colors have been swayed by perception, thanks to cultural conditioning—associating traditional gender roles and traits with masculinity and femininity.

Men, for instance, may be perceived as more competent or qualified for leadership positions, regardless of their actual skills or experience simply because they are believed to be more rational and objective because they're men. Women are generally considered more emotional and subjective and less likely to be able to "get things done."

This is similar to the perception that all men can fix a car, build or repair things, or know how to fight simply because they're men.

These role stereotypes have influenced people's perceptions *not just* of what it means to be a "man" or a "woman," but what it means to be a leader. Traits like assertiveness, confidence, and decisiveness are often associated with masculinity and leadership strength, while traits like nurturing, empathy, and collaboration are often associated with femininity and weakness.

This perception of women as "weak" is usually based on stereotypes and biases associating masculinity with strength, power, and authority.

Even if you're aware of the importance feminine energy brings to the table, research shows that unconscious bias and discrimination against women impact how others view their leadership abilities. Women may be judged more harshly for exhibiting assertiveness or dominance and may face more scrutiny and obstacles in positions of leadership. It's the old, "She's a bitch," if she is assertive versus "He's a strong leader," if he is assertive.

We need to explore our shadow, our unconscious thoughts, and intentionally deconstruct the stereotypes we hold.

A feminine leadership style emphasizes relationship building, inclusiveness, a focus on personal growth and well-being, and a more holistic approach to decision-making. It is "beautiful, graceful, nurturing, creative, and warm. There is power in being. There is power in silence."[1] Feminine power is focused on emotions, communication, compassion, and empathy, four qualities we may not initially think of as powerful. But, when we explore and implement them appropriately, they become a catalytic gestalt—a whole greater than the sum of its parts.

When paired and balanced with the male energy of doing, assertiveness, and aggressiveness, a third leadership style emerges —one that brings the best of both worlds—to the organization and world.

Until we are rooted in the feminine principle and uplifted from our cultural strengths, we cannot embrace the best leadership style —that is born of balance.

It's time to lead from a place of wholeness and self- (personal, collective, and ancestral) love. It's time to be reborn.

What is wrong with being empathetic, creative, relationship-oriented, and collaboratively focused while being strong and assertive when or as needed? This is the type of leadership that will hopefully lead to the rebirth of a nation.

See yourself now as the leader you are or can be—balanced, prioritizing relationships, collaboration, communication, and assertiveness.

This is a call to both women (and men) of color and the institutions that serve and/or employ them–to be effective conduits and catalysts of the type of leadership our society is knowingly and unknowingly aching for at this time.

Growing positive feminine power is an antidote to the skewed perceptions and use of power in Western society. We, personally, collectively, and nationally, will rise with the healing from a deeper, more respectful, and honoring focus on the feminine principle. This renewed mindset will feed a wholeness of reconnecting ideas, culture, and community through a balance of masculine and feminine.

The most personally powerful people and the strongest leaders of any age, color, or gender are those who embrace both their masculine and feminine power, knowing when to use which power to accomplish their goals.[2] For example, we may assign tasks, policies, or rules we expect our team (or neighbors or peers) to follow (operating from our male energy). Still, we can tap into our feminine energy to notice if someone is struggling and communicate with team members who raise concerns about a task or policy. We can also develop tasks and policies collectively.

Jenise, an exemplar of feminine power through leadership, has reflected on, practiced, and supported power-building in many ways. Her first doses of feminine power came through generations, through her family, and live through her today. With more examples of this energy, we can see the various power permutations and step into our own unique sway. As she reflects:

> Women who are making choices to see into someone's potential and then removing the barriers from their ability to succeed and move higher—there are countless women like that that I saw growing up. For me, that informed my understanding of what it means to truly lead.
>
> My great-grandfather died too soon. Without my great-grandfather, my great-grandmother and her children had to determine how they would adjust. They were sharecroppers, and the loss of my great-grandfather was pivotal. They packed up my family and moved to Milwaukee.
>
> My great uncle's wife died when my cousins were still young. My great-grandmother stepped in and helped care for my cousin while my uncle grieved. She also helped care for another cousin in need. She stood in the gap for so many of us. That was her power. She embodied the principle of using what is available to you to care for the most vulnerable among us. The children come first.
>
> My grandmother was one who had a very clear standard. I understood her standard; I also understood the love and the grace, the "good" in power, because of her.
>
> My mother exercised her power to make what seemed impossible possible. She raised my sister and me on her own. She was in early childhood education and, at her core, she's an advocate for children and a fervent believer in the power of education. While we were young, she worked to further her own career while raising two girls and working a full-time job. She didn't always have a babysitter. So, there were times when I would attend classes with her, quietly coloring in the back of the classroom.

She put us through Catholic school because she was insistent upon us receiving a good education. She couldn't afford the tuition so she volunteered for the church-sponsored bingo games in the evenings to help subsidize our tuition.

Through the pursuit of her own education and her efforts above and beyond to ensure my sister and me had a strong foundation, I learned to center possibility in the face of impossibility. I carry this with me now. When I'm told "no," I receive it as an invitation to explore other routes and an invitation to consider other ways I can reach the goal.

My godmother was another leader in my world who embodied possibility and creative power. She is an entrepreneur, artist, and the founder of an African dance company—one of the oldest in the United States. I always marveled at her ability to create. From the dances she has choreographed to the company she built, her power still endures today. She and other women I watched growing up created institutions for my community. I was surrounded by love and vision in abundance.

In deepening our feminine power, we can balance out the exaggerated masculine power that presides today. Well-balanced power is dynamic, flexible, and principles-driven, as Jenise explains:

When I consider power in the feminine principle, groundedness comes to mind. It's caretaking of the present, informed by our past and in consideration of the future's interests—past, present, and future all woven together. I see communities of women loving and honoring each other, caretaking for children together, serving as a balm for each other.

Power, when wielded correctly, is grounded in love. Power that is sought after or leveraged for the sake of personal benefit is power misused. That is completely antithetical to what I believe is the more transformational form of power, which is communal. It's in balance and shared. It is not one sided. It's informed and multi-faceted.

It is power with and not power over. Power distorted is power wielded over someone for the sake of personal benefit and gain versus what is in the best interest of the whole. That's why I believe and trust women in leadership. The women in my life have operated from an interest in what is best in the future, in the rising tide that lifts all boats.

We each have power characteristics that are filled with potential. These can be activated, and we can tap into power to ignite, start, and persist. Power used positively comes from within, from the examples around us, and the rules we see, understand, or dare to change.

Using balanced masculine and feminine power for good requires ongoing self-reflection, awareness of the potential impact of one's actions, and a commitment to making choices that prioritize the well-being of others and the greater good.

We can't swing from one extreme to the other, the male energy to the female, and hope to heal. That is not balanced, and it hasn't worked so far for anyone. The challenge for all of us will be to accept, welcome, and implement a balance.

No. It won't be easy, and it won't happen overnight. But it will happen as we persist in our vision and evolution.

The Power of Community and the Collective

Feminine power is essential for fostering the most potent type of power—that which is in the collective. Collaboration and cooperation can lead to the creation of more power, benefiting multiple parties simultaneously.

Jenise's sense of power was shaped by the collective from the beginning. She remembered her neighborhood being both magical and powerful, but even that had its shadow:

> I was raised in Milwaukee. I grew up in a neighborhood that has been labeled the most incarcerated zip code in the United States. But I never saw or perceived danger. I never understand my neighborhood to be anything other than home.
>
> My childhood was joyful. My neighborhood was magical to me. I lived directly across the street from my school. I went to one of the few Black Catholic Schools in Milwaukee. We had a Black male principal at a time when that was almost completely unheard of. I had a mixture of nuns and Black women who were my teachers. And every adult I encountered in the school had the highest expectations of success for me and my peers.
>
> All my friends that I went to school with lived in the neighborhood. They were some of the sharpest, kindest, most beautiful group of people that I ever encountered.
>
> My family lived nearby. If I walked this way, I would get to my father's mother's house. If I walked that way, I would get to my great-grandmother's house and my great uncle's house. My world was made up of about eight square blocks, and that world was magical to me.
>
> We had a magnolia tree in my backyard. When that tree bloomed, everything came to life. It was joyful.
>
> I come from a community that was overlooked. People assumed the worst about us, but I was surrounded by people who believed in the power of education, that we had the capability to do and be anything that we set our sights on.
>
> One day, I was volunteering to stuff envelopes for an annual appeal. I was around eight years old. Folding letters, placing them in the envelopes—it was all very exciting. The adults I was

with were reading off some of the addresses and one of them remarked, "Whew, 53206, that's the ghetto."

My little ears, not registering their meaning, perked up, "Oh, 53206. That's my zip code!" I was full of pride because I knew my address. That's a big deal when you're small. But when silence fell upon the room, I knew that phrase—"ghetto"—had a negative connotation to it. There was something negative that they were associating with my neighborhood, where I was from.

I felt ashamed about where I lived for the very first time in my life. I didn't understand. Why didn't they understand how beautiful it is? Why would they think that about my neighborhood?

Shame transitioned into anger, fury, and indignation. "Well, you don't know what you're missing. My neighborhood is magical. It has magical people in it," I thought.

I understood how that power of my community and the people in it worked in my own life because they equipped me with the ability to succeed regardless of what anybody thought about me or where I was from. It also seeded in me an insistence that no child should ever feel like that. No young people should ever feel that way.

My job in this lifetime is to ensure that young people don't feel the barriers from other people's perceptions about what they can be, about where they're from, what they have the capacity to achieve. That should be up to the young people. It shouldn't be up to anybody else.

Jenise's childhood was a foundation for how she used power as she came to be the person she is today. Given her rich community experience, she was able to activate and uplift communities as an adult. As she offers:

There was another older gentleman by the name of Carvis Braxton. Carvis came up in the '60s as an organizer. These two older men, well into their 60s, were running this organization, and here I am, a 20-year-old trying to change the world. They were so wonderful to me. They taught me, but also let me loose to flex my muscles and practice what they were teaching me.

There was a big project, and the organization was charged with developing a large-scale community strategic plan. They allowed me to take the reins of that community plan.

The first thing Carvis told me was, "You can't move a stitch until you meet at least 100 people in this neighborhood." I went out and literally knocked on all the doors in that neighborhood to meet people.

I met and I sat down with residents in their homes and got to know them. Carvis taught me that people don't move until they are angry. Not only do you have to know about what makes them joyful, you've got to know what they're not comfortable with. That's a form of power you won't find in the classroom. It comes from relationships with people who understand power and how it works.

I got to know this neighborhood. I got to know its people. I got to know the business owners. I got to see the power to influence up close and personal. I fell in love with it all so much that I moved into the neighborhood. I was a resident until about nine years ago. It still feels like home.

I got to know the residents. I pulled together a resident council to drive this strategic planning process. We met regularly over the course of a year. What came from those meetings was a powerful plan that was indicative of residents' needs, residents' desires, residents' aspirations for the neighborhood, and a clear articulation of the commitments and resources that would be necessary to move the plan forward.

We called into account the city, the alderwoman, and the county supervisor for the area. I'm so proud of that plan, the collaborative efforts of the resident council members, and the projects that were funded and moved forward as a result. I'm proud because it was a product of love, genuine love. It wasn't my voice. It wasn't Sherman's voice. It was the people's voice. It was the voice of power of, by, and for the people.

I've had older men who saw into me and said, "Go. Go forth." That was the masculine power urging me to act. But there was the feminine too—nurturing power.

That's the kind of power that I'm interested in practicing. One of the things that made me fall in love with Public Allies is that the organization offered a language and framework to pull together all these different principles that felt right and true.

One of them is that leadership is not positional. Leadership is an action. It's not a position or power to be wielded over. They are actions that many can take on behalf of the whole.

The best form of power is communal. It is about actions on behalf of the many, by the many and is shared.

I saw the movie *The Color Purple* when I was 14 and then I read the book. I often think about Celie's ability to exercise authority and love for herself in her life. I think about how the women who surrounded her helped her identify and uncover her sense of power, her authority in her life.

We all go through moments where we don't feel powerful. It's the women surrounding us who hold us up when we can't hold ourselves up, who remind us of who we are. Women linking arms with each other, saying, "It's okay. Even if you trip, I'm still holding you up. I've got you. It's okay. Until you regain your step, it's okay. I've got you. We've got each other." That's what I see.

Power can be harnessed to uplift communities, champion social justice, advocate for marginalized groups, and effect positive changes at all levels, formally and informally. It is the intent and actions of those wielding power, not power itself, that determines its impact. In fueling collective power, Jenise offers some words of wisdom, and some questions:

> You see who has the potential and you provide a platform for that talent to emerge. This is power not for personal gain but power for the sake of the collective, what's in the best interest of the whole.

> You don't walk alone. You walk with. Leadership is not positional. Leadership is about what you do, it's about the choices that you make. It's about what you do and how you do it. I believe we walk in leadership, and we walk in leadership together. Who is with you? Who is beside you in this leadership walk? Who are you carrying with you?

> Are you walking with ancestors or people in the present realm? Who is walking with you, and how do you continue to honor the fact that you're not walking alone?

Purposeful Power

Using power for good can be personally rewarding as well. It brings personal fulfillment and a sense of purpose to know and see that our actions are making a positive difference in people's lives. Aligning with one's values can provide a deep sense of satisfaction and contribute to a meaningful life.

With this mindset, we can wield power to move and shape ourselves, our relationships, our organizations, and our communities. We can create a new way of being or even a new structure or society. We can liberate ourselves from the metaphorical chains this society places on our minds and hearts.

When we think from these different levels—our inner world, people around us, our organizations, communities, and the broader systems—we can tap into power in ways that can liberate all of us. We must first be aware of and intentional with our power, and the power of others. It begins one person at a time.

The way we see leadership is to use power in a way that includes fostering empathy and compassion. It means considering the needs and experiences of others and working towards their well-being. Positive power helps people cultivate a sense of empathy and use their own power to uplift and support themselves, as well as those who are marginalized or vulnerable.

Using power for good on all levels helps build trust and foster collaborative relationships. When we use power responsibly and with integrity, we establish a foundation of trust. This foundation of trust builds a culture of trust, which in turn enables people to work together towards common goals. By working together toward common goals, we engender unity and cooperation and create better conditions for everyone.

Chapter 11: Using Power for Good

1. What does power mean to you, and how do you use it responsibly?
2. How does doing good align with your values and actions?

Jenise Terrell

As CEO of Public Allies, Jenise Terrell (she/her) brings over 25 years of experience in nonprofit leadership, community development, and leadership development. Jenise began her journey in leadership as a Public Allies AmeriCorps member herself in 1997. Throughout her more than 20-year history with Public Allies, Jenise has held several roles, including ally mentor and supervisor, field operations leader, fundraising strategist, government relations lead, executive vice president of program strategy, and most recently, interim CEO.

Jenise's personal mission is to create a world where all young people have the opportunity to realize their full potential. She has worked to fulfill that vision by leveraging national service as a vehicle to create pathways to leadership for marginalized and disenfranchised voices across the US. Jenise played a central role in developing innovative Public Allies initiatives: DREAMCorps, the first national service program to engage DREAMers (young adults with deferred immigration status) in national service; a collaborative, multi-city venture with the My Brother's Keeper Alliance to build career and education pathways for men of color, and a multi-city partnership with AARP designed to increase livable communities for multiple generations.

Jenise is a native Milwaukeean, a proud Public Allies Milwaukee alumna, a Marquette University alumna, and a working mother of two beautiful children. She is passionate about the history of Milwaukee's Black community, speculative fiction, and the writing of Toni Morrison, Alice Walker, Octavia Butler, N. K. Jemisin, and the legion of Black women who dare to tell the truth about our history and imagine a future where we all are free.

Chapter 12
Using Power for Positive Societal Change

My dad worked in a factory. One time his fingers got pressed in one of the machines, and he was injured. Thankfully, he didn't lose his fingers or break them, but he was hurt.

Seeing that he didn't want to make a big deal about it or make a complaint about it because he was afraid to lose his job—a job that was difficult for him to get—was maddening.

Even now, I hear stories of people who are still in that same place. It just brings so much of that anger to witness people be dehumanized in that way. My dad felt like he couldn't take that time off or wasn't worthy of taking time off because of fear.

I remember these incidents as a child, and they, unfortunately, still happen to people that I meet. It's those sorts of things that shaped me as a young person and fostered a lot of the anger and resentment that I felt.

I knew that I wanted to be involved in changing things, but I didn't fully know or understand my place in that. I was searching for it.

— Irene Romulo

Societal change begins with an awareness of inequity—often from those like Irene, who are impacted the most by it. Those impacted the most often feel the most powerless to change it when we are, in fact, the ones with the most power and ability to do so.

Experiencing the brunt of socioeconomic or political oppression can feel hopeless. It angers and frustrates us—even driving some to violence, to quitting, to walking away from the situation without attempting to change it because we don't believe we can.

WOC often forget the immense power we have within and its potential. It's like having a winning lottery ticket with a million-dollar payout waiting for us to just name it and claim it. Because we've never won more than a few dollars, we don't bother to check the numbers. The money is there, waiting on us to wake up and take it. We have power. We just haven't realized it yet. We are all powerful people.

When we "play small," we buy into a misconstrued notion that we don't have power. We wrongly believe that others have power, but not us. That lack of self-awareness, that lack of vision to claim and embrace our power hurts us and, inadvertently, others.

What BECOME has realized through many interviews and our work with WOC and others, is that the reason many WOC often abdicate or fail to grasp our power is born from adversity—be it systemic oppression or interpersonal harm. It's a carefully placed and disguised veil, nearly invisible. It colors our sight and skews our notions. It keeps us from seeing our potential, our beauty, and our potency.

But we can remove it. We have that power as well—the power to open our eyes and hearts to see ourselves and others clearly.

Some of us have recognized this power, and others haven't. Once we know we are powerful and that power is a tool shaped by intent, we are poised to be a cause for change. In short, we can create the reality we want and need, and the reality many around the world, and throughout history, have—once they recognized it was possible.

Power can show up in many ways—in our words and voice, through our decisions and the way we embody time, in the ways we share and show our talents, and through how we share or spend our resources (our "time, talent, and treasure").

Through our minds, our knowledge, and our awareness we can choose to leave our power dormant or neutral, or we can activate it and direct it toward goals, dreams, and visions. The decision is up to you. Will you play big, or will you play small?

The Power of Emotion

Emotions are an often-untapped source of power. They can create momentum or point to needed moments of stillness and reset. They can bind people together and be the music that guides our dance in unison.

Anger is one such emotion that can spark action, as Irene, a driven and triumphant servant leader, has experienced firsthand. As Irene describes:

> I was very angry in high school. I attended a predominantly Latinx school. I was involved in sports and AP [advanced placement] classes, but I always felt like there was a lot of inequality in the types of resources that we were given and the resources that I saw other schools have when we would travel for competitions.
>
> I was on the track team and saw the state of our track compared to, what seemed to me back then, world-class stadiums at other schools. I was in AP classes, so I was often pushed by my teachers to do well. I knew that even in our limited high school, I had access to some of the best classes they were able to give.

But I saw friends that I grew up with and hung out with after school be put in the core classes, which were lower-level classes. They weren't treated as being worthy. Their brilliance and talent were overlooked.

That fostered a lot of my anger. I didn't have the language or the analysis to understand how these things were systemic, so I bottled up a lot of my anger. I didn't know what else to do with it then.

Like a hammer, anger and power can be used for good or for evil. For instance, a hammer can help to build a house or be used to hurt a person. It's all in how you wield it since power is a tool that will mold to one's intent.

What many of us often forget or don't realize is that anger, when properly channeled, can be positively powerful. Anger can generate the motivational force we need to initiate action and address injustices or problems.

When channeled constructively, anger can fuel determination and drive people to take a stand, advocate for change, or work towards a positive cause.

We can create, influence, and shape institutions, our communities, and our society. All we need to do is wake up to this possibility with our mind, body, and behavior, says Irene. As she expounds:

I woke up to my power, to the possibility of power after spending decades angry at the systemic abuse I experienced. I was angry over the abuse my parents experienced and that created a desire in me to do more, and I have.

Everyone from my family—that I know of—is from the state of Guerrero, Mexico, which is in the southern and very hot part of Mexico. I was the oldest of two siblings. I have one younger brother. We grew up in Logan Square [a neighborhood in Chicago] in the '90s, back when it was predominantly Puerto Rican and Mexican communities.

When I was in middle school, we moved to Cicero, where I live now. My parents have been here ever since. I've lived in different places but at some point, I decided I wanted to come back home and be around family. Also, politically I felt it was important to be here.

I wanted to work and see change happen in the place where I grew up and knew there were a lot of issues to address. I've been here since then. In different ways and different capacities, I have dedicated myself to addressing injustice.

There has been pushback for the direction I've chosen and the choices I've made—sometimes from my parents. As the child of immigrants and being the eldest, I think they had a specific view of what I was supposed to do, and I wasn't doing it.

I think that view is shared by a lot of immigrant parents. The kids are supposed to go to college and become rich somehow and get our parents out of poverty. I'm interested in protests and work that doesn't necessarily pay much.

I've addressed that with them, and we've gotten to a place where they understand me, and I understand me.

Even amid personal (or sociopolitical) pushback, we can still drive for what we know and feel is right, given our power. It can be so easy to fall over, to succumb to social or familial pressures to give up or go in another direction. The power of purpose can give strength in these cases. When you have a clear goal and passion, and you know it's rooted in truth, let that fuel you.

I spoke English and was going to school. Only as an older adult did I realize how shared this experience is. I had a lot of responsibilities to help my parents out as their translator, reading things for them or helping them make decisions. That was leadership. That was power, but I didn't see it that way then.

I didn't have the words to describe it at the time, but I remember feeling angry at the way that things were or the ways that I would see my parents treated.

Back then, my parents were undocumented, and I heard the ways that they talked about the different harms they experienced at work but were afraid to speak out for fear of being arrested or deported. I heard about family members passing away in Mexico but saw family members here not able to travel because of their citizenship status.

When I went to college, I felt the same way. I often felt ostracized where I was. I sought things outside of my university to help me understand.

My life changed when I went to California and saw that organizing was a thing. I worked with an anti-militarism nonprofit addressing US militarism in other counties, as well as another nonprofit.

It was not just organizing that I was introduced to, but organizing that was led by predominantly queer, trans, Black, poor, and undocumented people.

The things that we were facing were wrong. There's not something inherently wrong with us, but there's something wrong with the way that the system is, and we can do something about it.

Those solutions can come from us. It's not a thing where we ask to be given the power to change, it's a thing where we have the power already, and just need to access and implement it.

Using Power for Positive Societal Change

We must be careful with power, though. While anger is a catalyst, it can also be a destroyer. It reminds me of the Hindu deity, Kali. She's a goddess of love but she's a destructive force. She destroys so that a new creation can emerge. Anger can dismantle but it can also deconstruct us, from the inside out, if we're not aware.

When pushed by emotions like anger, our vision can become blurred, and we can end up inadvertently carrying on the same things we want to change. Irene recalls:

> I knew I wanted to make a difference. I just didn't know how. I remember wanting to be a doctor and go to Africa. Or go back to Mexico and help the poor. I had that savior mentality because I knew there was injustice, I knew there was wrong, but I didn't know how to address it.

> Being in a space where people were allowed to be themselves and lead and hold leadership and push for change helped me understand the kind of power that I had, what power was possible, and what I wanted to do and be involved in.

> That's when I understood it's not about this savior stuff. I can't save anybody, and nobody is going to save me. I learned about the racism that's inherent in that sort of mentality.

> It's about transforming ourselves as individuals and working together to transform the reality around us. It's possible and it doesn't have to be around this concept of saving others.

> I'm so blessed to have had that opportunity to do that. That was a pivotal moment in my life.

As Irene learned, there's a difference between a savior mentality and a supportive mentality. While the intention to help others is often well-meaning, a savior mentality can be detrimental to both the person with the savior mindset and those they seek to save.

A savior mentality involves a strong desire to rescue people from their problems, often at the expense of their own well-being or boundaries. A person with a savior mentality may feel a sense of superiority or self-importance or the need for validation through their role as a helper or savior. They may overstep others' boundaries, disregarding the autonomy and choices of others in their attempt to "save" them.

A savior mindset can perpetuate dependency, undermine personal growth and autonomy, and contribute to an unhealthy power dynamic in relationships.

Anger and fear can perpetuate the savior mindset. Our movements cannot be solely fueled by anger. This motivator must evolve. It must transmute into a higher frequency energy.

By examining one's motivations, establishing healthy boundaries, supporting empowerment, and encouraging autonomy of others, we can support, activate, and move *with*, not save. Irene experienced this shift and urges others to reflect and move as well:

> I feel like a lot of the things that I've done begin with the anger that I feel with the way that things are, but then evolves into something else.
>
> In California, I learned to accept my ability to change things and the power that we each have. I was able to see how people can come together and do something together. We don't have to be alone. It can be transformative for us.
>
> The reason why I returned to Cicero was because I felt like I wanted to be in the place where I grew up and I knew that there was injustice happening. This feels like the place for me.
>
> I think it makes it possible for more people to step up and realize that we deserve more and be willing to figure out a way to be engaged. Many of our parents moved to Cicero because it was

the place where it was possible for them to, for the first time, purchase a home.

They feel comfortable here. There's a lot of other people who speak their language and have stores with their food and the items that they find comforting.

Our parents came here looking for that stability and a place to call their own. In a way, it is. But in a much bigger way, it isn't because it's a place that harms us. It's a place where there are so many things that are polluting our air and harming our health.

It's a place where we're not allowed to be in the decision-making spaces to pass policies that would benefit us or add more support systems.

Through writing, organizing, creating wedges, and building paths, we can make life better for all of us and those coming after.

To me, that means being rooted in a specific place and building with the people that are here. I no longer feel this desire to run away and be elsewhere.

I can support other people in other places and the work that they're doing without necessarily having to go and have this mentality of being a savior or having to be there myself. I can trust that I'm building work here that is supporting others somewhere else.

Irene went from a motivation to saving people elsewhere, to focusing on home, from having a more independent mindset, to supporting and being interdependent with fellow neighbors. Sometimes, in the individualistic culture in the US, it's easy to get stuck in individualism, to think we can be the hero. We can forget that a supporting role is just as powerful as the spotlight. We all need support and those that support us–our friends, family, community, neighbors, therapists—shape our identity and movement. To change society, we need to recognize all the different roles we and others can and need to play. As Irene expounds:

> People can come out of the shadows and find their space to be themselves and, even if afraid, be willing to be courageous and speak truth to power; make demands for what we deserve.
>
> I've had different roles in supporting that work. One of those was being the communications person for a while, so I was responding to reporters or journalists and trying to bring more attention to our work.
>
> I was angry about how undocumented communities and organizing communities were being portrayed in the media and the way that sometimes journalists would reach out to us and be like, "We need a crying mother who was separated from her children at the border. We want to interview them."
>
> I was seeing so much of our trauma be the center of attention because it's what drives clicks, or it's what will make the headline, or seeing pictures of migrants crossing on the cover without their permission. It's the way this dehumanization happens in journalism that drove a lot of my anger.
>
> One article from the *New York Times* took the 911 calls of people who were stranded in the desert as they were crossing. Most of those people eventually perished.
>
> They took those recordings, and you heard their desperate calls for help. That felt like such a violation of these people to me. To the *New York Times,* this is what is considered worthy of publishing. It's taking their moments without permission and presenting them as soundbites.
>
> I decided, "Why can't we be the ones that use the media?" We can be the ones that are reporting our own stories and writing our own narratives.

Using Power for Positive Societal Change

I was working on a project here in Cicero and looking at the library archives and seeing so much of what occurred here in the '60s and '70s with the race riots. How much of that was written from a white perspective and missing the voices of the Black people who were being persecuted in this town?

Now, this town is over 90% Latinx. To not read about them in these archives, is like, "What the heck?" That's when I decided to switch. I decided to be a journalist and started learning.

I was blessed to meet people in this town who had the same vision and noticed that there was a big gap. We decided to found our current organization, *Cicero Independiente*. That's where my journalism started.

Sometimes we find our sense of purpose and sometimes a sense of purpose finds us. When purpose meets power, magic happens. We create movement and contour reality to the shape of our vision. Irene fell into her purpose. Driven by anger and seeing the pain and injustice, she connected in unexpected ways. She found her sense of purpose (or it found her) and anger began to turn into hope. She used her power to create narratives, shape minds, and tell her own community's story.

I see journalism as a tool for liberation. There's so much power that comes from being able to narrate your own story, to be able to advocate for the issues that you care about. I'm a big fan of writer and abolitionist organizer Mariame Kaba.

One of the things that I heard her say and then read about her saying was we need to write ourselves into history. Otherwise, we will be erased and forgotten.

I see our journalism now and what we're doing with the paper as crucial to those future generations that are to come. I want people to read about our struggles and our organizing and the fact that we existed, and we were here.

I want people to know we didn't take things sitting down. We were doing something. I want them to read about it directly from us, in our voices, and to document all of what was happening—not just the struggle and not just the organizing, but the stories that existed or the amazing, brilliant things that young people are doing.

In 2020, when we saw all the uprisings across the world, here in Cicero we saw uprisings too. Unfortunately, they mirrored the anti-Black uprisings that happened in the '60s, especially on June 1.

One of the things I'm proud of is that we went out there. But we also understood that we're not just a camera. We are humans and we are people and we can't just stand by and watch as shit happens around us and people are beaten.

We went out there and intervened in things that were happening. We documented as much as we could. Then afterward, there were a lot of solidarity marches that emerged and solidarity movements and work that has been happening ever since. We documented that as well.

It took us a long time because we didn't want to be like other newsrooms that went right ahead and published something that was incorrect or unfinished.

We worked on a series to document that whole week as a way to uplift the organizing that occurred and the people that were leading that, while also holding a mirror to ourselves.

We may be a majority community of color now, but that anti-Black racism has not gone away. We need to address it. We need to do something about it.

We got a lot of support from people who were glad that we did that and affirmed their experience of what happened. A lot of the people in power, even the police, denied a lot of what happened, even though we had images and pictures of what occurred.

It was important in that sense. We also got a lot of hate from people saying, "How dare you write about us like this? Do you know how bad this makes us look?" This is what happened. This is what we did. This is an opportunity to change.

When making societal change, we must acknowledge and address mindset—the individual and collective consciousness. Irene does this by holding up a mirror to the beautiful and the ugly parts of systems, groups, and communities. Mirrors are so important. We can't see ourselves unless we have some sort of reflection. This goes for our minds and our collective behaviors as well. There's so much we don't see, even in our own minds, unless someone holds up "a mirror." We can welcome mirrors, and we can be mirrors for others and for society. Irene offers more examples:

I'm proud of the different pieces that young people have written exposing their culture and different groups and things that we're doing here. We published an article about low-rider culture in Cicero, which is not something that I was even aware of.[1]

Another pivotal piece we did was in 2021, about the use of gang contracts at the high school level. They are used to criminalize young people.[2]

High schoolers read it and emailed me. They asked me to be on a Zoom call with them so that they could question me about it. They asked me, "How did you find out about this? How come you know about this, and I don't? I'm a student here. How did you write this?" They were grilling me.

I like that. I like that it sparks people to think, act, and learn about things that are happening, but they may not necessarily know about.

Even with that investigation that I published, I got emails back from people who were affected by that. They are adults now and wrote to me thanking me for writing it. There was one man who wrote and said, "I always felt like I was the bad kid, or there was something wrong with me. I didn't realize that this was happening to others."

The Power of Love

When anger moves to hope and to love, magical things can happen. Our voice can inspire others, it can heal, it can spark positive change. It's okay to be wherever you are right now—be it angry, sad, fearful, or joyous. But know that this is just a state, and it will change. Also know that anger doesn't heal; the release of anger does. Love heals, joy heals, peace heals. As we heal, we can be in a better position to help the collective heal as well. As Irene adds:

Yellow is a hopeful color. That's something that I hope I never lose, even in moments where it's very hard. I'm hopeful that we are going to have a different future, and that's what we're working towards.

Ever since I was little, my favorite color has been yellow. Even though there is no yellow in my house, and I don't necessarily wear a lot of yellow, I love looking at the color yellow. I think it came from the yellow Power Ranger.

I always felt like the yellow Power Ranger was often overlooked in the show. I felt like she was overlooked and not as popular as the pink ranger, even though she was very intelligent and strong. She played an important role in taking down some of those monsters.

Sometimes, I've felt like I've been overlooked. Yes, as an individual, but also because of who I am and the community that I live in. I feel like we've been overlooked or not taken seriously. We're not accepted for everything that we are.

I now understand that my anger can be a driving force of motivation, but what truly sustains me is the love and compassion that people are capable of sharing within their communities. In movements and other creative endeavors that I admire, love has been the seed that blooms into something beautiful.

Love gives me patience even when it's hard to stay calm or be kind. I strive to care for others, even if I don't always like them because they're part of my present and future.

That same love fuels me to summon courage when I'm afraid, to speak up when it's uncomfortable. I recall a particularly nerve-wracking budget hearing. I was there as a journalist, with questions to ask, yet I still felt anxious. I gave myself a pep talk beforehand: "It's alright to feel scared. These things aren't easy, but I must try."

These people aren't used to being questioned or having somebody speak up. I told myself, "You love yourself. You love your mom, and you love your community. You deserve to have these things and you deserve to ask the questions. You're going to go and ask them."

It wasn't as bad as I thought once I was there. I said what I wanted to say, and I asked my questions, reminding myself that I see that love in myself and in other movements and spaces—people guided by that love that allows things to flourish and blossom.

Love is one of the most powerful forces in this universe, the seen and the unseen realms. When we move through pain, anger, desire, and even hope, we can experience the fruits of pure love. We, at BECOME, have love as one of our core values for this very reason. Love shifts, binds, heals, unifies, uplifts, and elevates. If we want to have a more unified society, more peaceful and just cities, states, and nations, love is essential.

We know that love heals psychologically. It can even heal physically. When applied to communities, it helps heal there as well. The community is an entity, a body of sorts, with the various elements influencing and affecting each other as well as the health of the whole. In societal level change, the collective must be seen as a body in addition to all the different parts.

Irene went on this journey from anger to community and wondrous change happened. When communities come together, they can transform conditions and shift consciousness. As Irene offers:

> I've lived here most of my life now. It's not to say that organizing hasn't been happening or there's never been people who have tried to change things in this town. But it's important to note how much in the last four or five years I've seen people harness the power within themselves to find others here and attempt to change things.
>
> It's been so wonderful to see the intergenerational part of it. People are reaching out to our elders. Our elders have faced a lot of challenges and tried to speak up but were shut down, but they have not given up. They're still trying.
>
> Seeing young people out and engaged now creates an expansive movement. They're all using their skills and their specific interests to build something different. There are gardening and trying to get access to food and justice and clean air and trying to change things in that way. Others are working with artists and using art. Some are trying to get involved in getting people elected who are more reflective of the values that they want to see.

Using Power for Positive Societal Change

I see this as an example in Cicero of how movements can be created with just a few people starting out and being like, "Hey, something is wrong. Something is happening. Let's do something," and bringing in others and giving people that courage to speak up and to intervene in their own ways.

Carla is one of the elders in the community. Since she moved here in the '80s, she's been outspoken and has named the harms that the schools and government is causing. Often, it's just the one voice.

She has made it possible for people to have the courage to speak up and to do something. She has put them in touch with the power they didn't know they had and has shown them how to access and use it.

In recent years, there have been a lot of younger people that have taken up her call and joined her in their own ways, bringing in their own viewpoints. I've seen that she's learning about pronouns and why we need to respect people's pronouns.

She's been learning more about trans issues. She's a very Catholic woman and is very guided by her faith and religion, but she understands when things are wrong, even in her religion and the spaces where she needs to learn and take a step back and listen.

There's a young person named Gracia who is a brilliant artist. Gracia brings so much joy to spaces and often reminds us to take care of ourselves, slowing down and making sure that we're showing care for each other and ourselves even in moments of grief—asking us what we need and bringing us food.

Carla is somebody who is like, "We don't have time! We need to show up! We need to protest and do something!" Seeing Carla learn so much from Gracia and Gracia taking up Carla's fight and shaping it to what we need now and including so many of the other things that Carla may not think about at first.

I see so much strength and so much power in that—not ignoring our elders but being open to sharing with them and loving them. It takes both.

I'm somebody that knows both of them, and I also watch them from afar. I'm always in awe of them. As part of what I've seen, those are two people—not the only ones—who despite being nervous and fearful about speaking up and repercussions that they might face, have been brave to show up at places and board meetings where they don't traditionally expect people to show up or say anything. They have shown up and are unapologetic about their demands and sharing what is needed.

I've been on both sides, as the organizer and the reporting side. Now, I'm trying to document what they're doing and elevating that. They make it possible for me to be courageous in those spaces.

Cicero is a place where our parents made a home, but now we're really making it our own and making the demands of things that we need. For example, during the pandemic, Cicero had some of the highest COVID-19 cases, but it wasn't until much later that Cicero had a testing site. It was after we had to fight for them that we got more testing sites through the community health centers. We saw the opening of roads of possibility—not to just be surviving, but to be thriving and create different alternatives and things that are really about supporting our well-being.

That's what is made possible by seeing the ripples of people, and people speaking up and standing up to those who have been in institutional power for so long.

These wins and realizations led to wisdom for all of us who are emerging and hopeful liberating leaders to embody in our everyday lives and change efforts. This wisdom and path to liberation is about moving in concert, together. It's about how to shift collectively and how to think about the group as well as all the people in it. As Irene shares further:

> When we find our truth and are doing stuff that we love, we can all be shiny and bright stars.
>
> We should also be moving toward building constellations and entire universes of a bunch of shiny bright stars that are creating different life, different things. That's the goal. How are we creating and building these shiny universes of a bunch of stars rather than a shiny star here and there.
>
> We don't all, for example, need to be writers. We don't all need to be the one who feels comfortable being on the podium or giving the interview to a TV and news network.
>
> I've witnessed how possible it is for people of different abilities and skills to step into those roles and how important and crucial they are. We need all sorts of people and all sorts of things. Making space for that is important.
>
> I would not have been able to do this alone. Everything that I've ever done has been done with other people. All the best things that I've ever done and all the best things that can be done are done in communion with others.
>
> I've been able to do what I've done because I've been in community and working with others. I've been learning from people who have taken all that anger, all that desire to see a different future, and put it into action, allowing that love that we feel for others to guide us.
>
> With Cicero, I see us as one of the ingredients. We were making something and it's just a small part of it. We need all the ingredients to make it possible. My role is building towards that. I'm glad I'm able to bring other people in and make space for them.

Even in the short time that we've been in existence, we've been able to see change in many of the young people we work with.

They told us that they finally feel like they have a place and their own purpose to work on themselves and what they want to do here in Cicero. Knowing that I was a part of making that possible is what my leadership is about.

Power, as a strategy to heal, begins with understanding that we are powerful beings, that the potential for power to develop is as real as the potential a caterpillar has to become a butterfly.

Bring two people, or even better, a community together and organize the power of the group and you'll have the power to change your society.

In our healing journey, power is essential. In our power-building journey, relationships are essential. In our journey to change society, community is essential.

Irene, like other contributors in this book, has learned that ultimately, a person who helps others reclaim their power does so by fostering a collaborative, uplifting, and trauma-informed environment. Political and socioeconomic change, indeed any kind of change, begins with our recognizing, claiming, and healing ourselves before tackling the issues around us. It can be a mutual event, but healing is our foundation. Without self-awareness and at least one foot on the healing path we cannot affect our desired change.

When we promote the autonomy, resilience, and self-empowerment of our friends, our families, and our communities while providing the necessary support and resources for their healing journey, we all benefit from the results. And when we do this together, for and with each other, we transform reality.

Chapter 12: Power for Societal Change

1. When have you felt most powerful, and how can you channel that for societal transformation?
2. What legacy of positive change do you want to leave for future generations?

Irene Romulo

As a co-founding editor of *Cicero Independiente,* Irene Romulo (she/her) has an impressive record of fellowships and activism, having dedicated her life to organizing with marginalized communities. She began her career as an organizer to end deportations and unjust treatment of people of color, which led to her work as a reporting fellow for the City Bureau in the past and later as a 2020 Voqal Fellow and an Ida B. Wells Fellow for investigative reporting.

Irene firmly believes that every life counts equally, and her commitment to bringing attention to the needs of marginalized communities is evident in her outstanding contributions to journalism. She has used her platform to document not only the atrocities often ignored by the mainstream media, but also the positive news about the progress of her community. Her work has strengthened marginalized communities' voices and inspired young journalists to follow in her footsteps.

With a fierce passion for equality and a drive to create awareness, Irene is an ideal role model and an inspiration for all of us. Her tireless efforts have been a reminder that even small efforts can make a massive difference.

Chapter 13
Power-Building Practices for Organizations

> Everybody has power. Power is not necessarily a feeling. We're all powerful. We all have the ability to influence.
>
> — Gabriela Garcia

For us, at BECOME, power within and power with are equally important, both for the communities we work with, as well as for us. We emphasize and fuel the collective's ability to influence and shape our lives, our communities, and broader society in a mutually beneficial way.

For our team members, power is personal, not just an abstract concept. Like many WOC, Gabriela grew up with conflicting ideas and experiences around power. Now with a PhD in educational psychology, Gabriela is driven by a commitment to advocate for the personal and professional power that transforms people, not just presents them with new skills. She believes integrating power into one's character leads to permanent, generational progress.

That's why her goals include nourishing communities that have been affected by poverty and injustice. Her upbringing, like all of us, shaped and, at times clouded, her views on power and the power within her. As she reflects:

> I am first generation Mexican and Guatemalan. My mom was born in Guatemala and my dad in Guadalajara, Mexico. They immigrated to the US separately in their late 20s and met in California. I was born in California and moved to Chicago when I was 12.
>
> I have a sister who is about five years younger than me. Because we moved around a lot within the Little Village neighborhood, I didn't have a sense of community growing up, expect for the general Latine community. We settled into our own house when I started seventh grade in the neighborhood of Gage Park.
>
> In addition to moving around a lot when I was younger, my mom also sheltered me and my sister, which limited who we hung out with and how much time we spent outside being kids. It didn't help that I was also a shy, timid kid growing up.
>
> When it came to power, my mom didn't explicitly instill that in me, as she would fight my battles for me and speak up for me. I didn't realize how much power I had as a developing person and how much power using my voice had until after my first year of college.
>
> I know now that there is also power in community. My love for community grew from seeing my parents, and seeing their love for their cultural norms, traditions, values, and ways of being. It was this that pushed me into learning more about my cultural background at an early age and connecting to the Latine community in Chicago.
>
> That's one of the passions that keeps me going in the work that I do and that's why it aligns—I value the importance of having a sense of community.

I'm a servant leader. I'm passionate about helping others and considering others and supporting them. I believe this comes from seeing how my mom operated within our family and out in the world—now I know or see that she exemplified masculine and feminine power by how she nurtured and protected what she cared about and loved.

We all grow up with various ideas of what power is and isn't. At BECOME, we've had several conversations on what power means to each of us. If we don't take the time to reflect and dig deep, our misconceptions and subconscious ideas of power will reign.

Some thought that power was evil or used to do harm. Others grew up linking power to violence or money. Some of us were taught that we should quell power, or that some of us have it and others don't. There are so many ways that power is presented through family, media, and in community, and those messages shape our definition and access to our own power.

We had to recognize that power is power—a neutral thing, like electricity or water, that can be used for good, bad, and neutral goals. We activate and use power for transformation and the realization of visions of thriving communities. But to spark power within community, we must first fuel it within ourselves.

Power can come through in various shapes and sizes. It can be assertive and full or open and welcoming. It can be busy or calm, moving or still. It can push or pull, embrace or repel. Given that many oppressed communities' ideas of power have been skewed, it is necessary to know how to activate and cultivate power in each of us, be it on a team or in a neighborhood.

On a personal level, BECOME has done this in various ways. Voice matters. Power comes through when one speaks with their authentic voice. Creating regular space for everyone's voice is a potent way to fuel each person's power.

Relationships are another vessel for power to shine through. When we ask questions, listen deeply, and mirror another's strengths and potential, it feeds the power inside.

For the purposes of activating and fueling leadership for WOC, counterbalancing the exaggerated focus on masculine power is essential in both organizational and neighborhood spaces. Feminine power is needed for true liberation and for the creation of different structures and a liberated society. Here Gabriela shares:

> I grew up seeing power, in general, in the context of the Latine culture. In terms of femininity, the feminine part is probably most connected to my cultural upbringing. It wasn't necessarily how I was raised, but I was very much aware that the women's socially constructed role in our household was nurturing and raising the children and making sure your husband has what he needs.

> I saw a little bit of that in my mom, but I also saw power in her in terms of making the final decisions in the household and being the one who "wore the pants" in the family.

> She had more of a partnership with my father versus my father being in a traditional family role. I've come to understand that I tend to have a very masculine energy or power, yet I can be nurturing and listen to and foster others. I also get to a point where I'm like, "We need to get things moving. We're talking about all of this. How are we going from A to B," in a direct and assertive manner.

> I'm still trying to make sense of how to balance that masculine and feminine power dynamic because I tend to lean toward masculine versus feminine power in different situations. How I use power looks different at work versus at home. At home, I can have a very feminine power with my son, but at work, I can have a very masculine power. My goal is to balance my power, so I use both wherever I am.

My passion around power is building as I see things like overturning *Roe v. Wade*. It's coming to an understanding of, "Wow. If we don't stand up and support each other, things like this will happen—ongoing attacks women." There's been a shift in that way, owning our power as women and not being apologetic for it.

I've learned that there are also power blockers like not being present or withholding your emotions or avoiding certain things, stress, or the tendency for perfectionism. I have some tendencies to want to be perfect in certain things. I was reflecting on this personal power weekend I attended recently and making the connection of the importance of the different types of power—feminine, masculine, generative, reactive, active, passive, affirming, and disaffirming. We need all these types of power to influence effectively.

Practicing things like meditation and journaling can help tap into these different types of power and see where your strengths and gaps are. I'm currently focusing on understanding how to embody generative and feminine power. When I think of feminine power, I think of nurturing, listening, inclusion, sharing, collaboration, and being in the moment.

I'm learning that the more you are yourself, the more authentic you are, then the more power you have. The more that you're able to not withhold your feelings and share what you have to say or are able to be present and engaged, the more power you have in whatever space you are in.

I try to remind myself of the importance of being authentic and keeping in mind those different types of powers and which ones I'm tapping into and which ones I'm not and really being reflective. I continuously ask myself, "Why am I not tapping into that kind of power?"

Power-Building Practices for Organizations

Power is power and power with integrity means following your values. Saying what you're going to do and doing what you say.

Shaping our power in feminine and masculine ways requires intentionality and practice. Collaboration, listening, and being present require practice. Creating that time and space in organizational and neighborhood spaces can provide the arena to grow purposeful power.

It's also helpful to name it. Name when you see positive feminine power in action. Name and interrogate your assumptions and biases of power and the different types of power to make sure you're not practicing power based on your assumptions. Gabriela offers further:

> BECOME is very much a collaborative space. Whenever I talk, I'm always mindful that I'm on a team, so I'll say things like, "We were thinking of this," or, "Correct me if I'm wrong, but we were talking about..." and doing a lot of fact-checking. We have cultivated that culture around acceptance and trying to be our authentic selves. Of course, it's still a work in progress.

Western society has placed power on the individual level as supreme. However, through *collective* power transformative societal change happens. Collective power on any scale can ripple out and create bigger waves.

At BECOME, we practice collective leadership for this very purpose. As mentioned previously, we're using sociocracy, a shared governance model, for honing collective power. Here, Gabriela reflects:

> We've really worked on a culture of inclusion, presence, collaboration, and nurturing. Ideas come up or different ways of thinking of things and there's room for those to grow. We've been creating and drawing from different power theories to

help us grow. We're implementing sociocracy. We have a strong focus on wellness. We have our personal peace days at the end of the month and a membership to a workout place in our building.

There's a lot of feminine energy in the way that we approach things. Feminine power is more holistic.

Since communication and collaboration are integral aspects of feminine power, we've included some tips on communication below:

- **Clarity and intent:** Clearly state the purpose and intent of the conversation at the beginning. Be specific about the topic or issue to be discussed to ensure all participants are on the same page.
- **Active listening:** Actively listen to the other person(s) involved in the conversation. Give them your full attention, show genuine interest, and avoid interrupting. Active listening helps show understanding and respect for the other person's perspective.
- **Clear communication:** Clearly articulate your thoughts, ideas, and feelings. Use concise and straightforward language. Avoid vague or ambiguous statements, slang, or jargon that could lead to misunderstanding. Use "I" statements to express your own perspective and avoid blaming or accusatory language.
- **Openness and honesty:** Create a safe and non-judgmental environment that encourages open and honest communication. Create and support an atmosphere of psychological safety—a place or space where all participants feel comfortable sharing their thoughts and opinions without fear of reprisal or criticism.

- **Empathy and understanding:** Practice empathy by trying to understand and appreciate the other person's viewpoint, even if you don't agree with it. Put yourself in their shoes and listen with the intention of understanding their perspective rather than immediately formulating counterarguments.
- **Seek clarification:** If something is unclear or you don't fully understand the other person's point, ask clarifying questions. Seek additional information or examples to ensure you have a comprehensive understanding of their perspective.
- **Mutual respect:** Show respect for the other person's ideas, opinions, and emotions, even if they differ from your own. Avoid personal attacks, defensiveness, or dismissive behavior. Treat each other with dignity and courtesy throughout the conversation.
- **Constructive feedback:** Provide constructive feedback when necessary, focusing on specific behaviors or actions rather than attacking the person's character. Frame feedback in a way that encourages growth and improvement.
- **Resolution and next steps:** Aim to reach a resolution or understanding by exploring potential solutions or compromises. Identify actionable steps or follow-up actions that will be taken to address the issue or move forward.
- **Reflection and follow-up:** After the conversation, take time to reflect on the discussion and any insights gained. Follow up with any agreed-upon actions or further discussions if necessary.

All power necessitates the education and implementation of the energy and awareness of feminine power, including:

- Encouraging the cultivation and use of intuition

- Integrating circle practice
- Using the language of cycles and collective practice, as well as openly exploring the feminine principle
- Being present with others
- Accepting what is
- Integrating contextual understanding
- Finding joy in the process versus being focused on the end result

Leaders who activate and utilize feminine power in themselves and encourage others to do the same practice these skills:

- Listening deeply
- Welcoming expression of others
- Facilitating connective dialogue
- Supporting the process of iterations in co-creation (leading cycles)
- Practicing social and emotional intelligence
- Mirroring other people, reflecting their power and potential
- Encouraging and uplifting others

By incorporating these elements into explicit conversations and beyond, we can achieve mutual understanding, address mutual concerns, and work towards productive and meaningful outcomes. These are ways for everyone to tap into their power together.

It's important to recognize that power is not a fixed or limited resource, but rather a dynamic and evolving force. Power, whether feminine or masculine, helps us shape our own narratives, challenge systems of oppression, and contribute to a more inclusive and equitable society. How we embrace it, use it, and work within it is different for each of us based on our place on our path.

So, the next time you see a teammate, a neighbor, or a friend or family member, consider that they are a powerful being, with some or much of their power untapped and unnoticed. Remind them that they have much potential and a wealth of strengths waiting to be uplifted, activated, and shine. Step into this space of potential and brilliance with them. Walk together as you realize the change you want to see.

Reflection Questions

1. How can leadership embody the balance of masculine and feminine energies?
2. What strategies can cultivate nurturing spaces that reflect people's personal power?

Gabriela Garcia

Dr. Gabriela Garcia (she/her) is unwavering and dedicated to promoting and nurturing communities affected by poverty and injustice and has committed over a decade to doing what she does best. Her extensive experience in evaluation and research design, qualitative methods, project management, theory of change and logic model development, and culturally responsive evaluation has proven to be a valuable asset to her and the communities she serves.

She has led or co-led mixed-method evaluations for numerous STEM and health initiatives funded by various federal and foundation organizations. Her areas of evaluation, research, and technical assistance work have included curriculum development, after-school programs, diversity, equity-focused initiatives, and broadening participation in STEM projects.

Aside from her extensive experience, Gabriela also actively presents her research and evaluation work at professional conferences like the American Evaluation Association, the Center for Culturally Responsive Evaluation and Assessment, and the National Latino Psychological Association. Her latest work, "Situational Awareness and Interpersonal Competence as Evaluator Competencies," has been co-published in the prestigious *American Journal of Evaluation.*

She is proud to hold a PhD in educational psychology with a program evaluation specialization from the University of Illinois at Urbana-Champaign. She is fluent in both Spanish and English. Gabriela is undeniably a force to be reckoned with in the world of education and research and one that stands out among the rest.

BECOME has been uplifted by Gabriela's commitment to integrity and accountability along with her profound passion for community voice, engagement, and collective power.

Afterword

BECOME is focused on people and communities BECOMING ... and that begins with one person—ourselves. Becoming, like healing, like growing, like discovery and leading, is a path, a journey through life.

The women in this book who have shared their stories, their failures and successes, and their struggles still face challenges. We never "arrive" but are always in flux, growing, learning, mentoring, and being mentored.

We're all at different places on our paths and like the childhood game of Chutes and Ladders, we can encounter trauma, tragedy, or new unexpected challenges no matter where we are on our path. None of us, for instance, could have anticipated what COVID-19 would be to us as parents, career women, partners, or individuals. The secret to becoming is to be aware of and work on the skills and things we can influence in our lives. This way, we're not only prepared but also can elevate and transcend even our own expectations.

On May 5, 2023, I brought the leaders of this book together to create a vision of what we hope for that's possible for us and the people and communities we all serve. Here's a brief look at the vision:

> We envision a transformative reality, liberated from fear, stifledness, and boundedness. People are born into a vibrant world, teeming with abundant and loving communities, where they are truly free to be their authentic selves. From the very moment of their birth until their final breath, their journey is marked by persistent care, wise guidance, and a profound connection to both the natural and spiritual realms. Every step they take is fueled by the boundless strength, power, and wisdom they inherit.
>
> Their lives are characterized by ceaseless exploration, relentless learning, and exponential growth, as they continuously unfurl the vast tapestry of their human and spiritual potential. They cultivate a profound sensory awareness that extends to the deepest corners of their being, including the intuitive whispers that guide them towards truth. The pillars of history, ancestry, and the sheer beauty of the present moment anchor them firmly in their realization of personal and collective liberation.
>
> Every aspect of society, be it people, media, education, or other institutions, effortlessly uplifts and reinforces this transformative reality. As a result, every soul is liberated to manifest their full brilliance, to radiate love unconditionally, and to navigate life's intricate dance with unwavering authenticity.

We hope you have been inspired or moved by the stories and information in this book. Consider sharing the book with others, and even creating sisterhood circles where you can journey together, looking inward to elevate yourselves and vision together so you can create your own utopia and place of peace, inspiration, and healing.

About Evaluation

"What works in solving big, devastating problems like structural racism, education inequities, and health disparities?" I asked my mentor, Debbie Salem, a community psychologist at Michigan State University, that very question when I was a junior in college.

She said, "It sounds like you care about evaluation." I was surprised to hear that there was a field of people who cared about solving significant issues like the ones I was deeply interested in.

Evaluation is a systematic process of learning and improving the impact of programs, projects, policies, or initiatives.

An evaluator's role is to gather data, conduct assessments, and provide objective and evidence-based analysis to inform decision-making. Through this data and analysis, we shape the effectiveness of what's being evaluated.

Professional evaluators often have expertise in evaluation methodologies, research design, data analysis, and subject matter knowledge related to the specific area being evaluated. We may work as independent consultants, within organizations, or as part of evaluation firms or research institutions. Our work contributes to evidence-based decision-making, program improvement, and accountability in various sectors, including education, healthcare, nonprofit organizations, and government agencies.

Understanding that evaluators help identify areas for improvement based on valid and reliable data and use appropriate analytical techniques to derive meaningful insights was intriguing to me; as was the realization these findings don't just end up in reports that gather dust on a bookshelf. The findings and reports provide recommendations and strategies to enhance program effectiveness, address weaknesses, or magnify strengths. They contribute to the continuous improvement of the evaluated programs or initiatives by tracking and informing progress and monitoring and guiding changes over time.

That was the beginning of my journey to becoming an evaluator. In graduate school, I studied under Dr. Stafford Hood, one of the forerunners of Culturally Responsive Evaluation. That grounded me in the need to start with culture and community and understand and respond to the sociopolitical context.

People have vastly different opinions and perceptions of evaluation. Some think it is merely data wrangling, like counting how many people were served by a program or how many meals or articles of clothing were distributed. Others may narrow it to tracking changes, like reading grades or arrests. It's so much more—it's living, breathing insights from real people that give organizations the informational power and data they need to affect change.

Evaluation is a tool for structural transformation and thriving communities. It can shape human action toward realizing a goal or vision, like the insights conveyed through this book. Evaluation can be the guiding light we need to analyze best what is working currently and excavate the truth about systems and human behaviors that shape our work and lives. Out of that truth can come new systems, structures, or conditions that work for the many versus the few.

On a deeper level, evaluators are equipped to surface the root causes of collective pain and poverty. To learn the actual effectiveness of something, we must look at what caused the impact, and the reason or contributors rarely consist of a single factor. Evaluators can do this. In Culturally Responsive Evaluation, we see evaluation as informed action toward justice and the benefit and activated empowerment of oppressed communities.

Given that most of our work is in and with communities of color, we have seen profound learning across several projects around women of color and our leadership. Three evaluation projects in particular directly examined programmatic effects or strategic engagement of women of color as leaders in their communities and formed the lessons learned for this book, including:

- **Public Allies** is a nonprofit organization that activates and uplifts young people from diverse backgrounds to become leaders and promote social justice and equity. They're a national organization with sites across the country providing support and recognition to those who have the potential to make a meaningful impact in creating a fairer society. Their Women's Leadership Project studied their impact on women's leadership trajectories.
- **Chicago Foundation for Women** was established in 1985 with the goal of increasing resources for women and girls. Its mission is to empower women and girls to become catalysts for building strong communities.
- **Cultivate** is a collaborative effort involving influential foundations in Chicago, including the Chicago Foundation for Women, Crossroads Fund, Woods Fund Chicago, and the Chicago Community Trust. Cultivate offers a platform for women of color community organizers and advocates to engage in group sessions centered around topics chosen by the participants

themselves. The program also provides coaching, leadership training, and spaces to cultivate networks and meaningful relationships among women of color.

About the Authors

Dr. Dominica McBride is a leading thinker in the realm of community psychology, community healing, and collective transformation. As a champion of Culturally Responsive Evaluation and a grassroots advocacy strategist, she has dedicated her work to building the capacity of communities to create the reality they desire and deserve.

In 2013, Dominica founded BECOME with the belief that communities should be at the forefront of realizing their visions of thriving communities. Drawing on her experience in program development and evaluation projects in Arizona, the Chicago area, and Tanzania, Africa and beyond, she recognizes the power of culturally responsive evaluation as a tool for positive change.

With a background in community psychology, Dominica has made significant contributions as a consultant, program director, adjunct faculty member, and therapist in the field. Her expertise and insights have made her a sought-after speaker and trainer for communities, coalitions, and organizations across the nation. She has also been recognized and honored with a range of awards for her outstanding work, including the Supervisor of the Year Award from the Chicago School of Professional Psychology and the Marcia Guttentag Promising New Evaluator Award from the American Evaluation Association.

Dominica holds a PhD in counseling psychology with a specialization in consultation from Arizona State University. Aside from her professional accomplishments, she embraces the joy of motherhood and finds fulfillment in witnessing her two remarkable children flourish.

BECOME

BECOME is a 501(c)3 movement-building and community transformation organization that facilitates grassroots community leadership and co-creates innovative solutions to help communities achieve collective liberation. We collaborate with organizations and neighborhood residents to develop sustainable solutions, expand community capacity to implement those solutions, and create lasting movement toward a shared vision. In this way, we nourish groups affected by poverty and injustice to build on cultural strengths and make their vision for a thriving community a reality. Our ultimate vision is a socially just world characterized by thriving communities, where residents, driven by love and resilience, uplift communal wellbeing, encouraging and actualizing collective growth.

Our collective transformation toolbox includes:

- Community engagement and facilitation: We use inclusive methods to facilitate group discussions and forums that foster collaboration and generate ideas.
- Policy and program development: We conduct community research and evaluation to develop innovative structures for social change.
- Community-driven strategic planning: We support communities to draw on collective wisdom to envision and create solutions.
- Training: We provide training on topics such as cultural humility and emotional intelligence to facilitate collective healing.
- Catalytic evaluation: We research, learn, and develop insights on the impact of solutions using a model that prioritizes social justice, cultural integrity, and collective learning and action.

Here's a list of our values and what we share with our partner organizations and communities:

- **Actualization:** Actualization is the intentional movement to fulfill one's human potential, living into one's highest, biggest self. For BECOME, we see this on the collective level as well. A community has interdependent potential that can be actualized with certain conditions, be it physical, emotional, social, and/or spiritual. We support our own and each other's personal and professional growth and see and support a bigger vision for and with other people and communities.
- **Love:** Love is consciousness and frequency. It's the interplay of thoughts, feelings, actions, and vibration. We believe that love exists within each person and all around us. It is also the web of active and metaphysical

care we give to ourselves and each other, the ways in which we perpetuate and support life and light.

- **Transcendence:** Transcendence is the ability to imagine, see, and create a situation or reality beyond the current. As much as we can imagine is as much as we can create. This involves hope, radical imagination, faith, and deep disciplined action.
- **Truth:** Truth is "that which is identical to being." It is layered. It includes each person's experience, the community and sociopolitical conditions that affect our lives, and the metaphysical reality around all of us. We are dedicated to seeing, speaking, and living out the truth.
- **Unity:** Unity is the underlying reality—*all* is one. We are interdependent, connected, and together, whole. This comes in the form of how we see one another. No matter how different we may appear, we need to see ourselves as each other - "I am because we are" or "I am you, you are me." We are interdependent with each other, with the earth, and with the cosmological reality around us.

Before You Go

You can make a difference.

Did you enjoy reading this book? Your voice counts and has the power to make a significant impact. Reviews play a vital role in an author's journey, helping to attract the attention of other readers and amplifying the book's reach.

By sharing your honest thoughts, you can help bring this book to the attention of fellow book lovers. Taking just five minutes to leave a review would mean the world to me. Your review can be as short as you like. You can get to this book's page on Amazon by typing in Dr. Dominica McBride, *Becoming Change Makers: The Exquisite Path to Leadership and Liberation for Women of Color.*

Once there, scroll down until you find the section that says "Leave a Review." Remember, even if you've only read one or two chapters, leaving a review is still valuable. Plus, Amazon allows readers to update their reviews at a later date if needed.

Finally, if you want to learn more about how you can get involved with BECOME, please feel free to reach out to me through email at dmcbride@becomecenter.org.

You can also learn more about our organization and other ways to support by going to www.becomecenter.org.

Thank you in advance for your kind support. Your feedback is immensely appreciated.

Acknowledgments

So many people, both past and living, have contributed to this book.

First off, I'd like to thank my mother for being the first strong WOC leader in my life. She's never seen herself as a leader, but she has taught me what resilience, strength, motherhood, unconditional love, and perseverance look like. My sister has also been an amazing support throughout this process and always.

Others who have made significant contributions to this work and who deserve standing ovations:

- Michelle G. Wilson, Becky Blanton, and the Networlding Publishing team. This book wouldn't exist in this form at this time without your talent and guidance.
- All the amazing leaders who were featured in this book. It would not be nearly as moving or substantial without your willingness to share your story and be the exemplars you are.
- The BECOME Team, including the amazing people featured in this book, as well Alicia Anderson for your energy, intentional and supportive collaboration, and compassionate evaluation. Big thanks to Scott Christian for your deep analysis, ever-present thoughtfulness and conscious creativity, Larry Washington for your deep support, accountability for joy, and willingness to help in

whatever way is needed, and Larry Barrett for your
critical and insightful observations and encouragement.

- The BECOME Board of Directors, including
  Revolution MacInnes for supporting BECOME from
  the beginning, Israil Thomas for your wise and constant
  guidance, and Rachael Marusarz for your insight, strong
  support, commitment, and tutelage.
- Dr. Tenia Davis for your support, ideas, friendship, and
  community. You were integral in bringing this to life.

Book Club Discussion and Reflection Questions

We hope that sisterhood groups are formed or strengthened through reading this book collectively and supporting each other in your leadership journeys. The following are prompts for reflection, discussion, and collective growth.

Chapter 1: Trauma and Resilience

1. Reflecting on your journey, how have you turned challenges into opportunities for growth?
2. How have your experiences shaped your story and inspired others?

Chapter 2: The Heart and Healing

1. What does healing mean to you, and what has it looked like in your life?
2. How can you nurture the healing you've experienced and take the next step on your journey?

Book Club Discussion and Reflection Questions

Chapter 3: Self-Love and Finding One's Authentic Voice

1. What are three things you genuinely love about yourself?
2. What part of yourself needs more care and tenderness?
3. What truth from your life do you wish to share with the world?

Chapter 4: Healing Practices for Organizations

1. Where have you experienced healing spaces—at home, in your neighborhood, or professionally?
2. How have (or could) you fostered moments of healing for others?

Chapter 5: The Importance of Relationships

1. How do your relationships reflect your values and support your needs?
2. In a tech-driven world, how do you balance personal connections with professional growth?

Chapter 6: Mentorship and Leadership Development

1. What have you gained from mentors, and what could you benefit from now?
2. What is your mentorship superpower, and how can you use it to guide others?

Chapter 7: Relationship-Building Practices for Organizations

1. In cultures that prioritize individualism, how can relationships take center stage?
2. How can you facilitate deeper connections within your community or organization?

Chapter 8: The What and Why of Intersectionality

1. List the identities you hold and reflect on how they intersect in your life.
2. How do (or could) you express your full self in different environments?
3. What would it mean to embrace and share your whole self everywhere?

Chapter 9: Cultural Self-Awareness

1. What have you learned about yourself or your community that inspires hope and strength?
2. Which moments of learning have shaped you, and who contributed to them?

Chapter 10: Intersectional Practices for Organizations

1. What did you learn by deeply listening to someone's story?
2. How can organizations create spaces that honor and respond to people's lived experiences?

Chapter 11: Using Power for Good

1. What does power mean to you, and how do you use it responsibly?
2. How does doing good align with your values and actions?

Chapter 12: Power for Societal Change

1. When have you felt most powerful, and how can you channel that for societal transformation?

2. What legacy of positive change do you want to leave for future generations?

Chapter 13: Power-Building Practices for Organizations

1. How can leadership embody the balance of masculine and feminine energies?
2. What strategies can cultivate nurturing spaces that reflect people's personal power?

Bonus Leadership Questions

1. How do you envision yourself as a leader?
2. What fuels your sense of purpose and leadership philosophy?

Notes

Introduction

1. "Social Relationships and Health: A Flashpoint for Health Policy," J Health Soc Behav 51, no. suppl (2010): S54-S66, doi:10.1177/0022146510383501 - https://www.ncbi.nlm.nih.gov/pmc/articles/PMC3150158/

1. Trauma and Resilience

1. "Sabu, James. "Human pain and genetics: Some basics," Br J Pain 7, no. 4 (2013): 171–178, doi:10.1177/2049463713506408. - https://www.ncbi.nlm.nih.gov/pmc/articles/PMC4590159/
2. Dr. Gabor, Mate. https://thewisdomoftrauma.com/
3. Janoff-Bulman, Ronnie and Hanson Frieze, Irene. "A Theoretical Perspective for Understanding Reactions to Victimization," *Journal of Social Issues* 39 (2): 1–17, https://doi.org/10.1111/j.1540-4560.1983.tb00138.x.
4. Maté, Gabor. "The Wisdom of Trauma,", accessed May 6, 2023, https://drgabormate.com/the-wisdom-of-trauma.
5. Uncovering the Trauma of Racism, Feburary, 2019. Accessed July 17, 2023. https://www.apa.org/pubs/highlights/spotlight/issue-128
6. Lanier, Paul PhD, MSW, "Racism is an Adverse Childhood Experience (ACE) - The Jordan Institute for Families," The Jordan Institute for Families (accessed August 20, 2021), https://jordaninstituteforfamilies.org/2020/racism-is-an-adverse-childhood-experience-ace/
7. Wade Jr., R., Cronholm, P.F., Fein, J.A., Forke, C.M., Davis, M.B., Harkins-Schwarz, M., Pachter, L.M., & Bair-Merritt, M.H. (2016). Household and community-level Adverse Childhood Experiences and adult health outcomes In a diverse urban sample. Child Abuse & Neglect, 52, 135-145.] https://pubmed.ncbi.nlm.nih.gov/26726759/
8. Kelly Campbell, "Healing Trauma: Why It's Fundamental for Effective Leadership," *Forbes,* May 9, 2022 https://www.forbes.com/sites/forbesbusinesscouncil/2022/05/09/healing-trauma-why-its-fundamental-for-effective-leadership/?sh=55cafffb2764.
9. Ibid.

2. The Heart and Healing

1. Thomas R. Egnew, "The Meaning of Healing: Transcending Suffering," *Annals of Family Medicine* 3 (3): 255–62, https://doi.org/10.1370/afm.313.

Notes

2. Michael Miller, "Emotional Rescue: The Heart-Brain Connection," *Cerebrum* (May–June 2019), www.ncbi.nlm.nih.gov/pmc/articles/PMC7075501/.
3. John Glenn Scott, Sara L. Warber, Paul Dieppe, David Jones, and Kurt C. Stange, "Healing Journey: A Qualitative Analysis of the Healing Experiences of Americans Suffering from Trauma and Illness," *BMJ Open* 7 (8), https://doi.org/10.1136/bmjopen-2017-016771.
4. Ibid.
5. Ibid.
6. Carl G. Jung, "Psychology and Religion." In *Psychology and Religion: West and East* (New Haven: Yale University Press, 1938), 131–93.
7. "What Is Santeria," Got Questions, accessed July 16, 2023, https://www.gotquestions.org/Santeria.html.
8. Ellen Barlow, "Spirituality and Healing," Harvard Medical School, January 14, 2015, https://hms.harvard.edu/news/spirituality-healing.
9. Ibid.
10. Heng Zhang, Nam Nguyen-Dinh, Hazreena Hussein, and Hong-Wei Ho, "The Effect of Healing Perception on the Visitors' Place Attachment and Their Loyalty toward a Metropolitan Park—Under the Aspect of Environmental Design," *International Journal of Environmental Research and Public Health* 19 (12): 7060, https://pubmed.ncbi.nlm.nih.gov/35742309/.

5. The Importance of Relationships on Every Level

1. Julianne Holt-Lunstad, Timothy B. Smith, and J. Bradley Lipton, "Social Relationships and Mortality Risk: A Meta-analytic Review," *PLOS Medicine,* July 27, 2010, https://journals.plos.org/plosmedicine/article?id=10.1371/journal.pmed.1000316.
2. Charles L. Ford and Larry J. Young, "Harnessing the Healing Power of Love," *Trends in Molecular Medicine,* August 4, 2021, https://www.cell.com/trends/molecular-medicine/fulltext/S1471-4914(21)00195-7.
3. "Ants on Peony Flowers: An Example of Biological Mutualism," University of Missouri Integrated Pest Management, May 29, 2018, https://ipm.missouri.edu/MEG/2018/5/antsOnPeonies/.
4. Emily Osterloff, "Mutualism: Eight Examples of Species That Work Together to Get Ahead," National History Museum, accessed July 16, 2023, https://www.nhm.ac.uk/discover/mutualism-examples-of-species-that-work-together.html.

8. The What and Why of Intersectionality

1. Katy Steinmetz, "She Coined the Term 'Intersectionality' Over 30 Years Ago. Here's What It Means to Her Today," *Time,* February 20, 2020, https://time.com/5786710/kimberle-crenshaw-intersectionality/.

Notes

2. Ibid.
3. Paola Rigo, Bindiya L. Ragunath, Marc H. Bornstein, and Gianluca Esposito, "Enlarged Group Effect: How a Shared Culture Shapes In-Group Perception," bioRxiv, accessed July 16, 2023, https://www.biorxiv.org/content/10.1101/2020.06.12.148601v1.full.pdf.
4. Yuan Cao, Luis Sebastian Contreras-Huerta, Jessica McFadyen, and Ross Cunningham, "Racial Bias in Neural Response to Others' Pain Is Reduced with Other-Race Contact," *Cortex* 70 (Sept 2015): 68–78, https://www.sciencedirect.com/science/article/pii/S0010945215000672.

11. Using Power for Good

1. "What Is Feminine Power and How Can We All Embrace It?" Wright Foundation, February 26, 2019, https://wrightfoundation.org/what-is-feminine-power-how-to-embrace-it.
2. Ibid.

12. Using Power for Positive Societal Change

1. Abel Rodriguez, "Lows Chicanos de Cicero," *Cicero Independiente,* September 7, 2021, https://www.ciceroindependiente.com/english/chicano-low-riders-cicero-cruising.
2. Irene Romulo, "'Gang Contracts' in Cicero and Berwyn Schools Raise Concerns About Criminalization of Youth, *Cicero Independiente,* May 26, 2021, https://www.ciceroindependiente.com/english/gang-contracts-morton-gang-database-cicero-berwyn.